James Graham

# The Whisky Taster

**Methuen Drama**

Published by Methuen Drama 2010

1 3 5 7 9 10 8 6 4 2

Methuen Drama
A & C Black Publishers Ltd
36 Soho Square
London W1D 3QY
www.methuendrama.com

ISBN 978 1 408 13004 9

A CIP catalogue record for this book is available from
the British Library

Typeset by Mark Heslington Ltd,
Scarborough, North Yorkshire
Printed and bound in Great Britain by
CPI Cox & Wyman, Reading, Berkshire

# The Whisky Taster

## by James Graham

*The Whisky Taster* received its world premiere
on 26 January 2010

The Bush Theatre would like to give particular thanks to: aka,
West 12 Shopping Centre and Westfield London; and would
like to thank Scott Rogers, Ben Hall, James Wannerton from
the UK Synaesthesia Association, Darren Rook & John
McCheyne from the Scotch Malt Whisky Society, Caroline
Eldridge, Guy Chapman at Target Media Group, www.urban-
office.com, Kiltsandallworldwide.com, Alex McColl at
MacKing and William Grant & Sons Distillers Ltd

# The Whisky Taster
## by James Graham

## Cast

| | |
|---|---|
| Barney | Samuel Barnett |
| Christopher | Chris Larkin |
| Malcolm | Simon Merrells |
| Nicola | Kate O'Flynn |
| The Whisky Taster | John Stahl |

## Creative Team

| | |
|---|---|
| Writer | James Graham |
| Director | James Grieve |
| Designer | Lucy Osborne |
| Lighting Designer | James Farncombe |
| Sound Designer | Emma Laxton |
| Assistant Director | Ant Stones |
| Company Stage Manager | Angela Riddell |
| Deputy Stage Manager | Anna-Maria Casson |
| Assistant Stage Manager | Harriet Stewart |
| Design Assistant | Fly Davis |
| Production Electrician | Jack Knowles |
| Costume Supervisor | Moi Tran |

# Company

### Samuel Barnett (Barney)

Theatre includes: *Dealer's Choice* (Menier Chocolate Factory/West End); *The History Boys* (National Theatre, international tour and Broadway); *When You Cure Me* (Bush); *His Dark Materials* (National Theatre); *The Marriage of Figaro* (Manchester Royal Exchange); *The Accrington Pals* (Chichester).

Television includes: *Miss Marple, Beautiful People (series 1&2), Desperate Romantics, Crooked House, John Adams, Wilfred Owen, Alexander Hamilton, The Royal, Strange, The Inspector Lynley Mysteries, Coupling.*

Film includes: *Bright Star, The History Boys, Mrs Henderson Presents.*

### Chris Larkin (Christopher)

Theatre includes: *The Lady from Debuque* (Haymarket Theatre); *His Dark Materials* (National Theatre); *Dark Corners* (Theatre Royal Windsor); *A Midsummer Night's Dream /Much Ado About Nothing* (Regent's Park Open Air Theatre); *When We Are Married* (Chichester Festival/Savoy Theatre); *Tess of the D'Urbervilles* (Derby/Salisbury Playhouse); *Getting On* (West Yorkshire Playhouse); *The Lucky Chance* (Derby Playhouse); *A Taste of Honey* (Theatre Clwyd); *Towards Zero* (Redgrave Theatre); *Taming of the Shrew* (The Mercury Theatre).

Television includes: *Marple: A Pocket Full of Rye, Doctor Who, Mysterious Island, Friends & Crocodiles, Rosemary & Thyme, Hitler: Rise of Evil, Shackleton (2002 BAFTA Winner: Drama Serial), Darwin, Roger Roger, Casualty, Highlander, Karaoke, Bliss, Frank Stubbs Promotes.*

Film includes: *Valkryie, After Thomas, Heroes & Villians, Master and Commander, Tea with Mussolini, Jane Eyre, Angels & Insects.*

### Simon Merrells (Malcolm)

Theatre includes: *On the Waterfront* (Theatre Royal Haymarket, West End); *Twelfth Night, Comedy of Errors* (RSC); *Much Ado About Nothing* (Liverpool Playhouse); *The Life of Galileo, Sing Yer Heart Out for the Lads* (National Theatre); *Frankie and Johnny in the Claire de Lune* (Nuffield Theatre, Southampton); *The Retirement of Tom Stevens* (Lakeside Theatre, Nottingham); *Romeo & Juliet* (ESC).

Television includes: *Ashes to Ashes, Doctors, The Bill, Family Affairs, Mersey Beat, Heartbeat, London's Burning, The New Adventures of Robin Hood.*

Film includes: *The Wolfman, Invisible Eyes.*

### Kate O'Flynn (Nicola)

Theatre includes: *House of Special Purpose* (Chichester Festival Theatre); *A Miracle* (Royal Court); *See How They Run, The Children's Hour* (Manchester Royal Exchange).

Television includes: *Kingdom, The Palace, Trial and Retribution, Heartbeat.*

Film includes: *Happy Go Lucky.*

### John Stahl (The Whisky Taster)

Theatre includes: *Troilus and Cressida, The Frontline, We the People, Othello* (Globe); *Macbeth* (Manchester Royal Exchange); *Carthage Must Be Destroyed* (Theatre Royal, Bath); *Ghosts* (Bristol Old Vic); *Mary Stewart* (National Theatre of Scotland); *The Crucible, Tamar's Revenge, Dog in the Manager, Pedro, The Great Pretender* (RSC); *The Alice Trilogy, The Weir* (Royal Court); *Blue Eyes and Heels, Angels and Saints* (Soho Theatre); *Professor Bernhardi* (Oxford Stage Company/Dumbfounded Theatre); *Bread and Butter, Sergeant*

*Musgrave's Dance* (Oxford Stage Company); *Crave* (Paines Plough); *Hamlet* (Belgrade Theatre, Coventry); *The Real World, The Baby, Paddy's Market, Sleeping Beauty, Gamblers, Macbeth* (Tron Theatre, Glasgow); *Anna Weiss, Shining Souls, The Architect, The Found Man* (Traverse Theatre).

Television includes: *Being Human, Beehive, Holby City, Rebus – The First Stone, Doctors, Murder Rooms, Glasgow Kiss*.

Film includes: *Loch Ness*.

## James Farncombe (Lighting Designer)

Theatre for the Bush includes: *2000 Feet Away, Tinderbox, tHe dYsFUnCKshOnalZ!, Crooked, I like Mine With a Kiss*.

Other theatre includes: *The Overcoat* (Lyric Hammersmith); *The Winter's Tale* (Nuffield Theatre and national tour) *Adolf Hitler: My Part in His Downfall* (Bristol Old Vic and tour); *The Great Game – Afghanistan, Not Black and White* (Tricycle); *Private Fears in Public Places* (Northampton Theatre Royal, nominated Best Lighting Design, TMA Theatre Awards, 2009) and *Breaking the Silence* (Nottingham Playhouse).

Upcoming productions include: *Ghost Stories* (Lyric Hammersmith) and *Dancing at Lughnasa* (Birmingham Rep). James is an Associate Artist at the Bush.

## James Graham (Writer)

Writing for theatre includes: *Albert's Boy, Eden's Empire* (winner of the Catherine Johnson Best Play award, 2007), *Little Madam, Sons of York* (Finborough Theatre); *Tory Boyz* (Soho Theatre); *suddenlossofdignity.com* (Bush); *A History of Falling Things* (Clwyd Theatre Cymru).

Writing for television includes: *Caught in a Trap* (ITV1).

Writing for radio includes: *How you feeling, Alf?, Albert's Boy* (Radio 4).

James is writer in residence at the Finborough Theatre and currently under commission with the UK Film Council.

## James Grieve (Director)

James is Associate Director of the Bush and Artistic Director of Paines Plough. Directing work for the Bush includes: *St Petersburg, Psychogeography*.

James co-founded the new writing company nabokov where he was artistic director for nine years. Directing work for nabokov includes: *Artefacts* (the Bush, national tour and Off-Broadway), *Kitchen, Bedtime for Bastards, Nikolina*.

Other theatre includes: *Country Music* (Royal Welsh College); *The List* (Arcola), *Old Street* (nabokov Arts Club), *Comfort* (Old Vic New Voices 24 Hour Plays). James has also directed comedians and performance poets including Isy Suttie, Simon Brodkin, Luke Wright and Aisle16.

## Emma Laxton (Sound Designer)

Theatre for the Bush includes: *If There Is I Haven't Found It Yet, 2nd May 1997, Apologia, The Contingency Plan, Wrecks, Broken Space Season, 2000 Feet Away, Tinderbox*.

Theatre for The Royal Court includes: *Tusk Tusk, Faces in the Crowd, That Face, Gone Too Far!, Catch, Scenes From The Back of Beyond, Woman and Scarecrow, The World's Biggest Diamond, Incomplete And Random Acts of Kindness, My Name Is Rachel Corrie* (also Minetta Lane, New York/Galway Festival/Edinburgh Festival), *Bone, The Weather, Bear Hug, Terrorism, Food Chain*.

West End theatre includes: *Treasure Island* (Theatre Royal Haymarket); *That Face* (Duke Of York's); *My Name Is Rachel Corrie* (Playhouse Theatre).

Other theatre includes: *Ghosts* (ATC at Arcola Theatre); *Pornography* (Tricycle Theatre/ Birmingham Rep/Traverse, Edinburgh); *A Christmas Carol* (Chichester Festival Theatre); *Welcome to Ramallah* (iceandfire); *Shoot/Get Treasure/Repeat* (National Theatre); *Europe* (Dundee Rep/Barbican Pit); *Other Hands* (Soho Theatre); *The Unthinkable* (Sheffield Theatres); *My Dad is a Birdman* (Young Vic); *The Gods Are Not To Blame* (Tiata Fahodzi at Arcola Theatre).

Emma is an Associate Artist at the Bush.

## Lucy Osborne (Designer)

Theatre for the Bush includes: *If There Is I Haven't Found It Yet,
Wrecks, Broken Space Season, Sea Wall, 2,000 Feet Away,
Tinderbox, tHe dYsFUnCKshOnalZ!*.

Recent theatre credits include: *Twelfth Night* for the Chicago
Shakespeare Theatre (for which she won the Chicago 'Jeff Award'
for Scenic Design); *Dreams of Violence* (Out of Joint); *Shades* (Royal
Court Young Writers Festival); *Macbeth* (Edinburgh
Lyceum/Nottingham Playhouse); *Nina* and *Gas Station Angel*
(repertoire, LAMDA); *Timing* (Kings Head) and *When Romeo Met
Juliet* (BBC).

She designed *Artefacts* (nabakov Theatre Company / Bush) and
*Some Kind of Bliss* (Trafalgar Studios), both of which transferred to
the 2008 *'Brits off Broadway Festival'* in New York and other theatre
credits include *Be My Baby* (New Vic Theatre); *Rope* (Watermill
Theatre); *Closer* (Theatre Royal Northampton); *The Long and the
Short and The Tall* (Sheffield Lyceum); *The Prayer Room*
(Birmingham Rep/Edinburgh Festival); *Ship of Fools* (set, Theatre
503); *The Unthinkable* (Sheffield Crucible Studio); and *Season of
Migration to the North* (RSC New Writing Season).

Lucy graduated from Motley Theatre Design School in 2003, having
also gained a BA in Fine Art from the University of Newcastle. She
is an Associate Artist at the Bush.

## Ant Stones (Assistant Director)

Ant has a BA (Hons) in English and Theatre from Warwick University
and is currently studying on the MFA in Theatre Directing at
Birkbeck.

Theatre as Director includes: *17 Hands* (Theatre 503/Slice); *The Red
House* (Warwick Arts Centre); *Under Construction* (ISTA festival, Sri
Lanka).

Theatre as Assistant Director includes: *If There Is I Haven't Found It
Yet* (Bush); *The Last Days of Judas Iscariot* (Arts Educational
School); *Shakespeare: Saints and Sinners* (Creation Theatre).

# The Bush Theatre

*'One of the most experienced prospectors of raw talent in Europe'*

*The Independent*

Since its inception in 1972, the Bush Theatre has pursued its singular vision of discovery, risk and entertainment from its home in Shepherds Bush. That vision is valued and embraced by a community of audience and artists radiating out from our distinctive corner of West London across the world. The Bush is a local theatre with an international reputation. Since its beginning, the Bush has produced hundreds of groundbreaking premieres, many of them Bush commissions, and hosted guest productions by leading companies and artists from across the world. On any given night, those queuing at the foot of our stairs to take their seats could have travelled from Auckland or popped in from round the corner.

What draws them to the Bush is the promise of a good night out and our proven commitment to launch, from our stage, successive generations of playwrights and artists. Samuel Adamson, David Eldridge, Jonathan Harvey, Catherine Johnson, Tony Kushner, Stephen Poliakoff, Jack Thorne and Victoria Wood (all then unknown) began their careers at the Bush. The unwritten contract between talent and risk is understood by actors who work at the Bush, creating roles in untested new plays. Unique amongst local theatres, the Bush consistently draws actors of the highest reputation and calibre. Joseph Fiennes and Ian Hart recently took leading roles in a first play by an unknown playwright to great critical success. John Simm and Richard Wilson acted in premieres both of which transferred into the West End. The Bush has won over 100 awards, and developed an enviable reputation for touring its acclaimed productions nationally and internationally.

Audiences and organisations far beyond our stage profit from the risks we take. The value attached to the Bush by other theatres and by the film and television industries is both significant and considerable. The Bush receives more than 1,000 scripts through the post every year, and reads and responds to them all. This is one small part of a comprehensive playwrights' development programme which nurtures the relationship between writer and director, as well as playwright residencies and commissions. Everything that we do to develop playwrights focuses them towards a production on our stage or beyond.

We have also launched an ambitious new education, training and professional development programme, **bushfutures**, providing opportunities for different sectors of the community and professionals to access the expertise of Bush playwrights, directors, designers, technicians and actors, and to play an active role in influencing the future development of the theatre and its programme. This Autumn saw the launch of our new social networking and online publishing website **www.bushgreen.org**. The site is a great new forum for playwrights and theatre people to meet, share experiences and collaborate. Through this pioneering work, the Bush will reach and connect with new writers and new audiences.

**Josie Rourke,** Artistic Director

## At the Bush Theatre

| | |
|---|---|
| Artistic Director | Josie Rourke |
| Executive Director | Angela Bond |
| Associate Director | James Grieve |
| Associate Director bushfutures | Anthea Williams |
| Finance Manager | Viren Thakker |
| Production Manager | Anthony Newton |
| Marketing Manager | Sophie Coke-Steel |
| Producers | Caroline Dyott |
| | Tara Wilkinson |
| Development Manager | Kirsty Raper |
| Development Officers | Bethany Ann McDonald |
| | Leonora Twynam |
| Development Intern | Charlotte Surman |
| Company Stage Manager | Angela Riddell |
| Box Office and Front of House Manager | Clare Moss |
| Assistant to the Directors | Liz Eddy |
| Box Office Assistants | Kirsty Cox, Alex Hern, Ava Leman Morgan, Kate McGregor, Amanda Ramasawmy, Lee Simpson |
| Front of House Duty Managers | Natasha Bloor, Kirsty Cox, Alex Hern, Annie Jenkins, Ava Leman Morgan, Kate McGregor, Amanda Ramasawmy, Jennifer Vile |
| Duty Technicians | John Gilroy, Vivienne Clavering, Ruth Perrin, Ben Sherratt, Dave Blakemore |
| Associate Artists | Tanya Burns, Arthur Darvill, Chloe Emmerson, James Farncombe, Richard Jordan, Emma Laxton, Paul Miller, Lucy Osborne, Hartley T A Kemp |

| | |
|---|---|
| **Associate Playwright** | Anthony Weigh |
| **Creative Associates** | Nathan Curry, Charlotte Gwinner, Clare Lizzimore, George Perrin, Hamish Pirie, Titas Halder |
| **Pearson Writer in Residence** | Nick Payne |
| **Press Representative** | Ewan Thomson |
| **Resident Assistant Director** | Ant Stones |
| **Intern** | Kirsty Patrick Ward |

The Bush Theatre
Shepherds Bush Green
London W12 8QD

Box Office: 020 8743 5050
www.bushtheatre.co.uk

The Alternative Theatre Company Ltd. (The Bush Theatre)
is a Registered Charity number: 270080
Co. registration number 1221968 | VAT no. 228 3163 73

## Be There at the Beginning

The Bush would like to say a very special 'Thank You' to the following supporters, corporate sponsors and trusts and foundations, whose valuable contributions continue to help us nurture and develop and present some of the brightest new literary stars and theatre artists.

**If you are interested in finding out how to be involved, please visit the 'Support Us' section of www.bushtheatre.co.uk, or call 020 8743 3584.**

**Lone Star**
Eric Abraham & Sigrid Rausing
Gianni Alen-Buckley
Catherine Johnson

**Handful of Stars**
Anonymous
Jim Broadbent
Clyde Cooper
David and Alexander
    Emmerson
Tom Erhardt
Julia Foster
Richard and Elizabeth Phillips
Alan Rickman
John and Tita Shakeshaft

**Glee Club**
Anonymous
John Botrill
David Brooks
Maggie Burrows
Clive Butler
Vivien Goodwin
Virginia Ironside
Neil LaBute
Antonia Lloyd
Michael McCoy

Judith Mellor
John and Jacqui Pearson
Mr and Mrs Alan Radcliffe
Radfin Courier Service
John Reynolds
Susie Sainsbury
Brian D Smith
Abigail Uden

**Corporate Sponsors**
The Agency (London) Ltd
Harbottle & Lewis LLP
Ludgate Environmental Ltd
Curtis Brown Group Ltd
West12 Shopping & Leisure
    Centre
Westfield London

**Trusts and Foundations**
The Daisy Trust
The D'Oyly Carte Charitable
    Trust
The Earls Court & Olympia
    Charitable Trust
The Elizabeth & Gordon Bloor
    Charitable Foundation
The Eranda Foundation
Garfield Weston Foundation

# bushfutures

bushfutures is a programme that allows our community and emerging practitioners and playwrights to access the work of the Bush.

## bushcontenders

Over 60 and love the theatre?

Nearly went for it but life got in the way?

bushcontenders is a new year round acting programme for everyone who could have been a contender. Members will receive discounted tickets to selected Saturday matinees and take part in an acting workshop with cast and directors here at the Bush following the performance. There is no charge for the workshop, all you need is to register in advance.

Bushcontenders for The Whisky Taster – 30 January

Missed it? Come to bushcontenders for Eigengrau – 20 March

## bushactivists

bushactivists is a group for young people aged 15–20 who live, work or study in Hammersmith and Fulham. Activists will have the chance to see what happens behind the scenes here at the theatre and receive a free ticket for one selected performance of each show at the Bush. On the day of the performance, Activists will take part in a fun pre-performance workshop before seeing the show as a group.

Bushactivists for The Whisky Taster – 27 January
Missed it? Come to bushactivists for Eigengrau – 17 March

## A Night Less Ordinary

Under 26? Like getting a freebie? Then you've come to the right place.

As part of a new Arts Council England scheme (in association with Metro), the Bush is offering free theatre tickets to those aged 25 and under (one free ticket available per person per year, subject to availability). So if you fancy A Night Less Ordinary and want to see some of the best new shows in London call us on 020 8743 5050 for more details and to book tickets.

### To find out more about bushfutures contact
### *bushfutures@bushtheatre.co.uk*
*or call Anthea Williams on 020 8743 3584*

# bushgreen

The Bush Theatre has recently launched
bushgreen, a social networking website for people
in theatre to connect, collaborate and publish
plays in innovative ways. The mission of bushgreen
is to connect playwrights with theatre practitioners,
plays with producers to promote best practice and
to inspire the creation and production of exciting
new theatre.

## bushgreen allows members to:

→ Submit plays directly to the Bush for our team to
  read and consider for production

→ Connect with other playwrights, directors,
  producers and theatres

→ Publish scripts online so members can access
  your work

→ Purchase scripts from hundreds of new
  playwrights

There are thousands of members and hundreds of
plays on the site.

To join log on to **www.bushgreen.org**

JERWOOD
CHARITABLE FOUNDATION

Strawberry Vale Productions in association with the Bush Theatre presents

## BY PENELOPE SKINNER

**10 MAR–10 AP**

# EIGENGRAU

[ay-gen-gr-ow] -*noun* intrinsic light; the colour seen by the eye in perfect darkness

**R**ose believes in true love and leprechauns. Her flatmate Cassie is engaged in a fervent struggle against patriarchal oppression.

Across London, Mark believes in the power of marketing. His flatmate Tim Muffin is engaged in a fervent struggle against his own waistline.

When circumstance throws them together, all four have their beliefs tested to devastating effect in a biting black comedy about trying to connect in a ci where Gumtree can sometimes feel like your closest friend.

**Penelope Skinner**'s previous writing credits include *F\*\*ked* (Old Red Lion).

★★★★★ **"F\*\*ked should be on everybody's lips"** TIME OUT (on *F\*\*ked*)

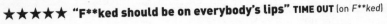

**Cast includ**
Sinead Matthew

**Direction** Polly Findl
**Design** Hannah Cla
**Lighting** Matthew Pitm

**Tickets** £9-£

**Box Office** 020 8743 50
www.bushtheatre.co.

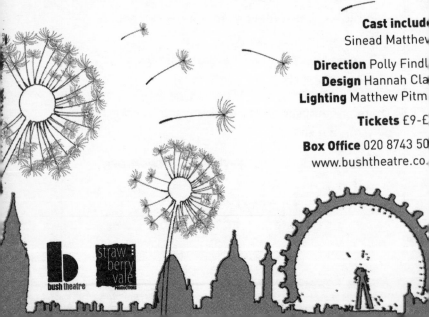

bush theatre

straw berry vale
PRODUCTIONS

# The Whisky Taster

## Characters

**Barney,** *male, mid-late 20s, North Midlands.*
**Nicola,** *female, mid-late 20s, South London.*
**The Whisky Taster,** *male, 70s, Scottish.*
**Malcolm,** *male, 40s, English.*
**Chris,** *male, 40s.*
**Scott,** *voice only.*


## A note on the text

A slash mark (/) indicates the character that speaks next should begin with their line.

An ellipsis (...) indicates hesitation. A dash (–) indicates a change in thought or broken speech.

(text in brackets) indicates a line spoken almost privately, to oneself, but still aloud (just).


## A note on 'characters'

Both **Nicola** and **Barney** sometimes speak through fictional characters or voices they have created, generally stereotypes, including 'Charles and Timothy' – city bankers; or 'Keith and Barry' – cockney geezers.


## A note on synaesthesia

A neurological condition where those afflicted can feel 'sensations' towards colours, shapes and patterns, or project colours onto objects such as days and emotions.

*The rooftop terrace of an advertising agency, central London. Distant sound of traffic below. The only colours evident are black, white and grey.*

**Barney** and **Nicola** *stand apart, facing each other.* **Nicola** *smokes.* **Barney** *wears a thick coat, his hands tucked into his pockets.*

**Barney**   Hope it does.

**Nicola**   What?

**Barney**   Snow.

**Nicola**   Do you? I don't, hate it.

**Barney**   Cold enough.

**Nicola**   You'd die, left out in the cold, you. Nothing on you.

**Barney**   I like it. Don't like / being too hot.

**Nicola**   Them little knees of yours, knocking together.

**Barney**   Thank you.

**Nicola**   (*giggles*) Knobbliest knees I've ever seen, yours are.

**Barney**   Oy, don't.

**Nicola**   What?

**Barney**   'What'? Having a go at me knees. I'm / sensitive about –

**Nicola**   What? You have got skinny legs, Barn'.

**Barney**   Why you telling me that?

**Nicola**   Good thing, that. / For some people.

**Barney**   I know I've got skinny legs, I see 'em every day. What people?

**Nicola**   Girls.

**Barney**   Well I'm not / a girl, am I.

**Nicola**   Some girls'd kill for them legs. I'd kill for 'em. And your figure, pretty much.

**Barney**   I . . . it – I don't know how to respond to that. Nicola.

**Nicola**   Compliment.

**Barney**   Bollocks was it.

**Nicola**   Was. Oy.

**Barney**   'You've got legs like a little girl'?

**Nicola**   I didn't say 'little girl', you did. I said you've got *little* legs, *like* a girl, / so don't –

**Barney**   I can't believe we're still talking about it. I can't believe I'm up here listening to you bully me, freezing my tits off, while you have a fag.

**Nicola**   What the fuck is wrong with you? Wrong side of the what's-it / or fucking what?

**Barney**   Nothing. Hate Mondays.

**Nicola**   What?

**Barney**   Hate Mondays.

**Nicola**   Uh, that's original.

**Barney**   Uh, not trying to be original. Just saying.

**Nicola**   (*beat while she smokes*) All right then, Picasso. Do it. What's Mondays?

**Barney**   (*beat. Shrugs.*) I don't . . . not all the same, is it, morning's different to –

**Nicola**   (*mock big sigh*) Oh. Ok. Well, what is right now, Monday?

**Barney**   Dunno, it's . . . I can't . . . It might be a bit . . . dunno. / Lilac?

**Nicola**   How long we got? – what? / Lilac.

**Barney**  Lilac. Yeah. But it . . . like, fades in and out. Tastes a bit . . . what was – shit, what were them awful purple, pink, sweets you used to get? Like *Refreshers* but not. Taste like soap, or potpourri (*pronounced as in 'pot-puree'*) or–

**Nicola**  Parma violets.

**Barney**  Parma violets! / Yuk, hate them.

**Nicola**  What, what did you just say? 'Pot' . . . did you pronounce it 'Potpourri'? / It's –

**Barney**  What?

**Nicola**  It's potpourri, idiot. (*Laughs.*) How did . . . ? / Potpourri?

**Barney**  That's how it's spelt.

**Nicola**  I don't care how it's fucking spelt, that's not how it's fucking said; / 'potpourri'.

**Barney**  Well anyway.

**Nicola**  Amazing. Not like you, / getting words wrong –

**Barney**  Whatever, I was talking, I thought we were / just talking –

**Nicola**  We are talking, we are just talking; fine, lilac. Fine. Bit like my shirt, / yes?

**Barney**  It's 'kind of' lilac. Monday morning. Be something else by this afternoon. Normally turns yellow into green, or . . . (*shrugs*).

**Nicola**  (*referencing her white shirt*) Actually it's more pink, this, isn't it? Oh I dunno, whatevs. Not sending you funny or nothing?

**Barney**  I have. Ways of. Controlling it. Sort of.

**Nicola**  How?

**Barney**  By not . . . I just. Like I just try not to think about your shirt being. Lilac. I just try not to . . . *see* it. So that I don't start getting all of those . . . erm. Feeling. Things.

**Nicola**   Well. (*Smokes. Deep breath.*) God, my stomach's spinning now. Nervous.

**Barney**   We'll be fine. (*Beat.*) Can't believe you had a go at my knees.

**Nicola**   Jesus.

**Barney**   Don't hear me saying anything about … your …

**Nicola**   What?

**Barney**   Your … I dunno, just –

**Nicola**   No, 'anything about my' what?

**Barney**   I can't think of anything.

**Nicola**   Awwh. Liar.

**Barney**   Seriously.

**Nicola**   So I'm perfect am I? Perfect in every single way.

**Nicola** *spins playfully.* **Barney** *shifts and stamps his feet.* **Nicola** *smokes.*

**Nicola**   You don't strike me as someone who does well in the cold, Barney, is all I'm saying. Is all I was Ob-Serv-Ing. Ok?

**Barney**   Still like it when it snows, though. I like it when I'm inside and I'm looking outside And It Is Snowing.

**Nicola**   Well it's cold enough. I bet it does.

**Barney**   I hope it does.

**Nicola**   Nobody up here, this morning. Never happens.

**Barney**   (*wrapping his jacket tighter*) Not surprised, fucking hell.

**Nicola**   See. You're going blue. I like your jacket, though. / Incidentally.

**Barney**   Oh. Really?

**Nicola**   Yeah, where'd you get it from?

**Barney**   Dunno, don't remember.

**Nicola**   (*groans*) Don't mean you're gay. Barney, just cause you remember where you get your clothes from.

**Barney**   I don't remember because I bought it last year. It's last year's winter coat.

**Nicola**   That's a bit of a faux paus, innit? Gonna get a new one?

**Barney**   You just said you liked this one.

**Nicola**   (*smokes*) We'd be about the first to know. I reckon. Up here. If it snowed. Bout the first to know in the whole of London, nearly. 'The first flakes'.

**Barney**   You about done with that? He's coming in at three, need to prepare.

**Nicola**   We are prepared. Chillax.

**Barney**   Don't say that.

**Nicola**   (*mock-Northern*) 'Don't say that'.

(*Smokes. Looks behind his shoulder.*) You know Centre Point. If it fell over. Kind of. Would it hit us?

**Barney**   (*glancing behind. Disinterested.*) I. Dunno.

**Nicola**   If it tipped like that. (*Demonstrates.*) Straight.

**Barney**   I don't think so. / I don't think that's –

**Nicola**   But if it did fall like that.

**Barney**   I don't think that's how buildings fall. If you look at –

**Nicola**   I know, but (fuck), I know, but if it did, fall straight, would it hit us?

**Barney**   No.

**Nicola**   (*smokes*) Heard Malcolm's gonna decide about Mumbai this week.

**Barney**   Really?

**Nicola**   Can't believe *he's* not just taking it. Idiot. That job; why wouldn't you?

**Barney**   Wish he was, Jesus Christ, imagine that. Him a thousand miles away, leaving / us to just . . .

**Nicola**   S'cause he's worried about not being here, I'll bet. The Execs fucking him over, getting rid.

**Barney**   Just gossip, it's all bollocks.

**Nicola**   (*as Barry*) Someone's gonna be jumpin' into his shoes, know what I'm mean, you get what I'm saying, kiddo?

**Barney**   (*as Keith*) Jump in his grave as quick, would cha, fuckin' 'ell, love, blimey.

**Nicola**   (*smiles. Smokes.*) Well. People talk. About you. One day. You know they do,

**Barney**   No they . . . as if I'd, as if I'd ever wanna be stuck in his . . . like some . . .

**Nicola**   Well. Whoever he picks for Mumbai, fuck me. What a dream. Just 'imaj' (*imagine*).

**Barney**   Could be you, never know.

**Nicola**   Oh OK Barney, yeah, they'd give me my own team, my own fucking. . . brand new –

**Barney**   Don't know why they're not picking two. Why would they want to split a pair up?

**Nicola**   Well I don't wanna think about it, no point. Beside, if it's either of us then it'd be bloody you, wouldn't it. So . . . there you go.

What if it is you? Drive you nuts out there, wouldn't it?

**Barney**   I don't . . . it's . . . I'm not even / sure I'd . . .

**Nicola**   Have you seen *Slumdog Millionaire*? You'd have an eppy.

**Barney**  (*checking his watch*) Are you nearly done?

**Nicola**  Chillax. / 'Don't say that!'

**Barney**  Don't say that. (Fucking Nora) …

**Nicola**  (*smokes*) Had my second fitting at the weekend, Barney-boy. Looking good.

You still bringing Joanne?

**Barney** *looks at his feet as he stamps them.*

**Nicola**  Barn, you –?

**Barney**  I thought the silence might be enough to imply that I wasn't.

**Nicola**  Oh. What happened?

**Barney**  Nothing.

**Nicola**  When?

**Barney**  Friday night.

**Nicola**  What was it?

**Barney**  Well, technically Saturday morning. But it was, uh … you know. Set in motion. Friday night.

**Nicola**  Mutual?

**Barney**  Yes. No. More me. But …

**Nicola**  She was a lovely girl, Barney. Really pretty.

**Barney**  I didn't love her.

**Nicola**  You didn't try.

**Barney**  You shouldn't have to try.

**Nicola**  You never try.

**Barney**  You shouldn't have to. Nick. (You shouldn't have to).

**Nicola** *singes the end of her fag with her lighter flame whilst she speaks, even though it doesn't need relighting. (A common trait.)*

**Nicola**   Parma Frickin' Violets. Yeah man. Would always have a couple rattling round the pockets of my blazer at school. Along with all sorts of shit. 'Laggie' bands. Ahuh.

You know at home, after school, did you watch CBBC or CITV?

**Barney**   CITV. Always. Better.

**Nicola**   Nah. CBBC. *Grange Hill*. *Blue Peter*.

**Barney**   CITV to start with, then flick over for *Byker Grove*.

**Nicola**   No way, Jose. CITV was a bag of wank.

**Barney**   Er, *Fun House*?

**Nicola**   Only one, though. Jesus, *Fun House*!

**Barney**   Saw him at uni, Pat Sharp. Came and did a night or something.

**Nicola**   'Ooh I'm Barney, I went to uni'.

**Barney** *mock-sighs and* **Nicola** *imitates him with an even louder mock-sigh as* **Barney** *does a louder one back. They smile. They do this a lot.*

**Nicola**   (*singing*) 'Fun House! It's a whole lot of fun! / Prizes to be won!'

**Barney**   (*singing*) 'Prizes to be won'.

**Nicola**   (*singing*) 'It's a real crazy show where anything can go!'

(*smokes*) Megadrive or SNES?

**Barney**   SNES.

**Nicola**   Knew you'd say that.

**Barney**   So. Knew you'd be Sega, so . . .

**Nicola**   Yeah. Better.

**Barney**   Except that it wasn't, though.

**Nicola**   Well, was, though, so . . .

**Barney** Sonic was shit.

**Nicola** What?!

**Barney** You could never see where you ... just tap some, some buttons really hard and somehow you bounce your way to the end of the level. / What the –?

**Nicola** 'Oh. I'm Mario. I go about one mile an hour. Hop. Walk. Hop. Walk. Oh no, a mushroom. Because I'm a plumber with a mushroom deficiency, for no reason ...'

**Barney** Not defic- ... it's an allergy. Deficiency means you need more, not less.

**Nicola** (*mock-northern*) 'Eeh, deficiency means you need more not less.'

**Barney** Why does your impression always sound so ... 'exhausted'?

**Nicola** Cause that's what northerners sound like. 'After a day down't pit.'

**Barney** Well. I'm not Northern. I'm ... Mansfield's Midlands. Technically. North Midlands.

**Nicola** Potato patarto. Where does the north start, then?

**Barney** It – I dunno. Yorkshire, maybe.

**Nicola** How far's that from you?

**Barney** Like ... twenty minutes, or –

**Nicola** There you go. Good as. (*Checks her watch.*) Fuck, better get down.

**Barney**: I told you.

**Nicola**: (*mock-northern*) 'I told yer'. (*Beat.*) Oy. Don't be weird.

**Barney**: Don't be ... what? Don't be –

**Nicola**: You know. Don't be the 'you' that's weird. Be the 'you' that's 'gifted'. Just today.

*Meeting Room. Black, white and grey.*

*A table. A pot plant in the corner.* **Barney**, **Nicola** *and* **Malcolm**.

**Malcolm** *fiddles with his phone a lot, so his level of distraction varies while talking.* **Nicola** *occasionally rearranges a bottle of vodka and some glasses on the table.*

**Malcolm**   Brown?

**Nicola**   Yeah, isn't he, Barn? On your face.

**Malcolm**   Really? God that's funny; rained the whole time.

**Nicola**   Oh did it? Oh no.

**Malcolm**   That's the ... haha, that's the thing, what I kept trying to tell everyone when they ... everyone's all like, 'uh ner ner, India over Christmas, lucky you', and I was a just a bit like, 'erm, what? Sorry, no, it's cold, and, basically the same as here, and, I'm looking ...' (*laughs*), you know, wandering around office blocks and fucking ...

**Nicola**   But good, though?

**Malcolm**   Yeah, no, no, no, yeah, good. Really good. Really great place.

You two all set, then? Annoying that he's late, but I wouldn't / expect anything less.

**Nicola**   Yeah, we're good to go, aren't we Barney.

**Malcolm**   Big one, this one. Be really ... not to be all (*mock screams*) 'aargh, pressure'. Huh. But, uh. But yes. If we get this, really great. Great for all of us, the company, you know, good for me, huh, my contact, certainly good for you. You pair. So ...

**Nicola**   No, we know, don't worry, Malcolm. We're on it. I'm leading the spiel this time.

**Malcolm**   Y ... right. (*Slight beat.*) Oh, right, you are?

**Nicola**   Yeah, my turn.

**Malcolm**   OK.

**Nicola**  (*pause.*) What's the place again? Me and Barn' tried to Google Earth it, but –

**Malcolm**  Chakala, it's called. / 'C-h-a …'

**Nicola**  Chakala.

**Malcolm**  Yeah, like North West Mumbai, it's… a lot of IT companies and, erm …

(*phone starts to ring*) Those call centres, you know.

(Oh God, what do you want?).

(*answers*) Hello? (*Waits.*) Hel -?

(*hangs up*) Fuck it. Erm. So yeah. Lucky boy or girl, whoever gets to run the show over there.

**Nicola**  Exciting.

**Malcolm**  Yeah, no, it is. And what with advertising here having been so … the past year, just, Jesus, whereas over there, it's just, the, the pace it's moving at, it's gonna be –

**Nicola**  Really? Is it?

**Malcolm**  – brilliant. Yeah. And you know, look, new decade now, and all that, plan for the future of the company. With you guys. (*Gestures them 'grandly'.*) 'The future'. Huh.

(*Looks at his watch. Sighs.*) Come on, getting silly now.

**Nicola**  (*rearranging the table*) So there's nothing else we need to know? About Chris? Christopher?

**Malcolm**  Uh, Chris. Actually, no Christopher. Oh I don't fucking know. But no, he's all right. Can be a little bit, erm … but he's all right. Honestly didn't really know him that well, thought he was a bit of a Hoorah to be honest. Always felt like he thought he belonged at Oxford or … had a thing up his … about red bricks; I mean it was fucking Manchester for God's … hardly erm …

What do we even call this one? Decade. The teens? Or what? The . . . ? 'The Noughties' never really took off, did it, as a name?

**Nicola**   I completely didn't realise we were in a new decade, for ages.

**Malcolm**   I know. / Strange, wasn't it?

**Nicola**   Think it was Barney / that told me.

**Malcolm**   Remember, like, '89 – well, you two probably . . . and '99, everyone looking back, defining everything, that, that kind of distinction between . . . but no, this one, no one really talked about it. It's like we're too old now. Haha. Can't be doing with celebrating. Or something. Or maybe we just didn't feel like it. This time. Maybe we just –

*Chris enters, offering his hand.*

**Chris**   Malcolm.

**Malcolm**   (*shaking*) Hey, Chris, you old devil / how you doing?

**Barney/ Nicola**   Hello.

**Chris**   Oh, God, I'm so sorry, bloody . . . taxis / round here just –

**Malcolm**   No that's all right. D'you get offered a tea or coffee / on your way up?

**Chris**   No, I'm fine. Fine.

**Malcolm**   Uh, this is Nicola. / 'One half'.

**Nicola**   (*shaking his hand*) Hello, all right?

**Chris**   Yes.

**Malcolm**   And Barney. The other half.

**Barney**   Hello.

**Chris**   I'm very sorry. Everything just / overrunning, you know.

**Nicola**   Oh God, no, / don't be silly.

**Chris**   The first one goes over and then it / … you know.
Knock on effect.

**Nicola**   It happens. Please. (*Offering the seat.*) Where have
you just come from? Not far.

**Chris**   Well. I … well, I can't really say, can I, so …

**Nicola**   Oh.

**Chris**   Well let me put it this way. Today is our … uh, you
know, what would you – our 'assault' on marketing.

**Nicola**   Right.

**Chris**   We're looking to invite three of the agencies we
meet to pitch a campaign and unless, huh … well, unless
you want me to give you the name of your competitors, the
people competing with you for this contract –

**Nicola**   God, no no no. I –

**Chris**   Well it wouldn't be very discreet would it? If I told
you where I'd been.

**Nicola**   Of course not, no. Absolutely.

**Barney**   Would you like a drink or anything?

**Chris**   No, thank you.

**Nicola**   They reckon it might snow later.

**Chris**   Really? Well, I'm just back from Minsk, so …

**Nicola**   (*laughs*) Right. Well.

**Chris**   You know. The snow there is …

**Nicola**   I can imagine.

**Chris**   … exactly. So …

**Nicola**   Well. Um. Well. First off, we love it. (*Chuckles.*)

**Barney**   (*chuckles*) Yes.

**Chris**  Good.

**Nicola**  I mean we would say that, of course. We want the job, but ...

**Chris**  And you're young, too.

**Nicola**  Ha.

**Chris**  Beer out of an ashtray and all that. Ahuh. / But, um ...

**Malcolm**  (*knowingly playful*) Well we were there once, Chris, need I remind.

**Chris**  I've no idea what's he's talking about, I was a model student. Malcolm, shush.

**Nicola**  Ahah, OK. Erm, so but yeah, we really do love this. We, both of us, after tasting it, just thought, 'wow', / so much different to –

**Barney**  So fresh and clean and –

**Nicola**  Yeah, exactly, fresh and crisp, we said, and clean, and so ... Our thoughts are ... we wondered about pitching this to a slightly higher demographic than you kind of indicated at in your brief. For the reason being, erm, well if you, for example, often if you position something as a classier product, and then after an initial period deposition it entirely – we're talking like over a two, three year campaign, then –

**Barney**  It's a strategy that we've seen work time and again mainly in rebranding –

**Nicola**  Right, a brand repositions itself higher, makes itself exclusive, a sense of, erm, of, like, the unattainable, so that when you deposition to the mainstream, open it up to everyone, people flock, because they're grateful.

**Barney**  *Marks and Spencer's*. Classic example; they were lingering in the, the depths of, of scuzziness, and so repositioned themselves *too* high, out of the woman on the street's reach, and then gradually began opening out again.

**Nicola**  We're seeing it happen now with *Waitrose*, it's happened a bit with *Prada*. / It's –

**Chris**  Right, but –

**Nicola**  Sorry?

**Chris**  Right, but . . . we're not rebranding, are we. We haven't even launched yet. / You can't, you know, you can't change people's mind about something they haven't even. . .

**Nicola**  Oh, of course, of course, no that's . . . yes, no I see what you're . . .

But thing is, we think, the problem with vodka over here, the way it's marketed and –

**Barney**  And the way it's consumed –

**Nicola**  And the way it's consumed, particularly the way it's consumed. If you go into any off-licence you'll see literally a whole shelf of very cheap-looking, cheap-tasting, uh, um, 'I'm-not-buying-it-for-the-taste-it's-just-to-get-me-fucked' kind of vodkas. All branded in those same colours, conjuring up all those images of . . . of . . .

**Barney**  Of wrong side of the wall, communist, / hammer and sickle –

**Nicola**  Yeah, Russia. Cold, industrial, really cold Russia. So what we're actually . . . I suppose what we're saying is that we don't just want to rebrand your vodka, we want to rebrand *Vodka* using yours as the, as the spearhead. Or –

**Barney**  A lot of young people, young *British* people, don't buy expensive vodka; why? Because they don't think of vodka as something you buy for the *taste*. Necessarily. It isn't wine or, or, or brandy, there's no culture of sampling it, enjoying different brands.

**Nicola**  It's a social thing.

**Barney**  It's stigma. It's –

**Nicola**    You mix it with coke, lemonade. Or make it taste like vanilla. Chocolate. It's a shot before you hit the town. For depressed tramps, for ... for Bridget Jones in between the bits with the men. But this? It's just ... it's really fucking good. Sorry. But it is.

**Barney**    It's too good. We think. For that. This is vodka ... at, like, a dinner party vodka.

**Nicola**    Sat out in the garden kind of vodka, or while reading a book. Opera vodka.

**Barney**    And that's how we would identify our campaign. Creeping into the public conscience gradually.

**Nicola**    So no huge full-page ads, bus banners, magazine inserts, nothing above urinals.

**Barney**    Spend a fortune on a TFL package? Get on every tube, every line? It's a waste. Domination packages, brand an entire station?

**Nicola**    No. Truly classy things don't shout at people. They whisper. Sorry to sound all Hoxton Square wanky, but ...

**Barney**    Nothing generic. Specific. Targeted. / Direct.

**Nicola**    Direct. Exactly. And our analytics department is ... well, it's what really puts us ahead of other agencies. The database, seriously, it can ... well, let's say, I don't know, pick a – gay? Manchester. We can list what TV shows, websites, what clubs, bars, you know, commuter lines. Uh, Black. Asian. White. Middle class. Middle age. Children. Obviously inappropriate for a, you know, a vodka drink but you get the idea.

**Barney**    So for example, once we pin our demographic down, we could tell you instantly that for, say, London transport we'd be best spending more on Victoria and Jubilee.

**Nicola**    Just sheer statistics. Just, it's, you know, / it's facts, just facts.

**Barney**   Maybe Piccadilly. I wouldn't think on the
Northern Line –

**Chris**   People ... sorry. People don't drink vodka on the
Northern line?

**Barney**   Well, no they do, and that's the problem. / Actually
*on* –

**Nicola**   Actually *on* the fucking Northern Line.

**Barney**   Phase Two, we can start thinking about banner ads
in newspapers –

**Nicola**   Like the *Guardian*, / maybe the *Telegraph* –

**Barney**   Further down the line, TV, say *Sky Arts*, say uh –

**Nicola**   *Film Four* –

**Barney**   But for now, forget it. Better a, a, like a guerrilla
viral campaign, plant a few *agent provocateurs* on Twitter,
setting up Facebook fan groups, begin to whip up a buzz
without having to spend barely a penny, reducing your
budget and also, over time, if we're brave enough, see an
increase in integrity *and* sales. Win win.

**Chris**   (*beat*) OK. Well. Obviously, you know, Malcolm's
portfolio speaks for itself and it's an ... an interesting idea.
(*Thinks.*) I have to say, though ... hmm ...

**Nicola**   Go on, it's all right.

**Chris**   A 'luxury' ... a luxury item? I just think, you know,
in these times of, of, huh, downturn and depression, isn't
making yourself seem luxurious and / sort of –

**Nicola**   No, OK, I do see / your point, but –

**Chris**   I mean, ha, I'm glad you like it so much but –

**Malcolm**   We all like it, Chris. I think / that's what Nicola –

**Chris**   But to make it 'exclusive', you know. That seems to
be / risking potential –

**Nicola**   It is a slightly, yeah, nerve-wracking proposition, sure, but it's what we do, and, and with us, our digital and print production, that's all done in-house / so there's no –

**Chris**   We-ell, so are most of the major agencies / I've been –

**Nicola**   And the colours! Barney.

**Chris**   The ... what's that?

**Nicola**   The campaign colours. As an example. Barn? (*Holds a glass of vodka out.*)

**Chris**   Oh. Well. We kind of already have our colours from the Baltic launch –

**Nicola**   No, trust me. He is brilliant at this.

**Chris**   Well as I –

**Nicola**   Barney?

**Barney**   (*unsure. Takes the glass. Sips. Beat. Solemnly ...*) Blue ... Silver ... and gold.

**Chris**   (*long pause. Studies* **Barney**.) That ... that's *perfect* ...

**Nicola**   Told you.

**Chris**   ... thank you.

Well. Erm. Yes, I mean, yes, of course, no question that we'll be wanting you to present to us a campaign. Uh –

**Nicola**   Awh brilliant, / cool. Thank you.

**Malcolm**   Thank you, Chris, that's great, / we'd be delighted.

**Chris**   Yeah, well, why don't you guys collect your ideas and things together and, let's say, what, week today, give us the lowdown?

**Malcolm**   No problem at all, look / forward to it.

**Chris**   Sorry it all feels a little quick, / it's just that –

**Malcolm**   Oh God, not at all, no. Barney? Could you ... show Chris –

**Barney**   (*going*) Oh, yes, of . . . uh, it, this way. Please.

**Malcolm**   Bloody good to see you again.

**Chris**   You too. (*To* **Nicola**.) Bye.

**Nicola**   Bye.

**Barney** *and* **Chris** *exit.*

**Malcolm**   So. Well done you.

**Nicola**   Oh. Well. Well done you. And Barney.

**Malcolm**   (*beat. Checks behind him; conspiratorially.*) Bit of a dick, isn't he? Chris.

**Nicola**   Ha. He was all right, bit up himself.

**Malcolm**   Don't even know how he got that job, used to be like this City . . . twathead, but. . .

(*beat*) So you reckon you'll lead on the campaign then, or . . . ?

**Nicola**   Uh, dunno, me and Barney'll talk about it. Doesn't really matter, we say 'lead', but, you know, with us two, like all the teams, / it's always –

**Malcolm**   Yeah. Yeah, sure.

How does . . . it is incredible, isn't it? Barney. Every time. How does he do it?

**Nicola**   I don't know. I don't like asking, do you know what I mean; don't like asking him to do it. Reckon it hurts him a bit or something.

**Malcolm**   What, like . . . (*beat*) What, do you mean that's not him . . . that's not even him going at full speed, kind of thing?

**Nicola**   Oh, no, no. He tries to keep a lid on it. That's why I don't like asking.

**Malcolm**   So . . . so he could potentially be even more . . . ?

**Nicola**  I dunno.

**Malcolm**  Because ... huh, you know, like I say, Nick, this one ... we could really do with getting this one. Ahuh. And if there's anything that we could do. Anything *you* could do. As team leader this round. You know. Be good opportunity, actually, for you. What with the Mumbai job coming up and everything. Nice little chance, well deserved. At last.

**Nicola**  ... r-right. (*Beat. Laughs, but tries not to.*) Erm. Right. OK.

**Malcolm**  Yeah?

**Nicola**  Yeah.

**Malcolm**  (*kind of mock-'go-getting'*) So we gonna win this one?

**Nicola**  Fuck a duck, yeah.

**Malcolm**  Great. That's fucking awesome.

**Barney** *returns*.

**Malcolm**  Whey, and speak of the devil.

**Nicola**  All right?

**Barney**  Yeah.

**Malcolm**  Nice work, Barney, good on you. Both of you. Excellent. So. Debrief. Thoughts? Thoughts on what seemed to land, what didn't? Let's really push this idea, yeah? Really ask questions of it, no surprises on the day, OK? I had some ... 'thoughts', if –

**Nicola**  OK.

**Malcolm**  Right, so let's just ... given, OK, given all that you were talking about, back there, about, uh, 'culture', the culture of drinking, what we drink, why we ...

(*beat. Thinks.*) I mean. You. What ... what makes you drink? Do you think?

**Nicola**   (*pause*). Erm ...

**Malcolm**   Because you do, don't you. Don't you? Sorry, this isn't a, a, a ... huh, I suppose I'm just saying–just asking ... because you do. People your age. More than nearly anyone ever, and ...

**Nicola**   Erm. Huh, I dunno. Barn?

**Malcolm**   OK. Forget that. Let's go back a step. Erm. The demographic, this idea of it being, uh, top end, of ... this luxury thing, some of which he seemed to get, other times ... I just wonder whether we're missing a trick.

**Nicola**   OK.

**Malcolm**   I just wonder whether ... whether it's not – this is gonna sound, huh ... but whether or not it's 'fairer' ... OK? ... to spread the net a little wider, to include people like you. Young people. Because you do drink, right? You almost 'have to', given, huh, well when you look around, what's happening, how fucked it all is for you, just – (*Mimes necking a glass.*) I just wonder whether a 'nice', and it is, a 'nice vodka' could benefit you lot. Dare I say, benefit you lot more. Instead of it being out of your reach.

**Nicola**   OK. OK, I do see what you're saying.

**Malcolm**   It's just, I'm just chucking things in. You know.

**Nicola**   No, no, no, yeah. I think it's just that –

**Barney**   I think because instead of being something you 'need', something to, erm ... 'down' in order to distract you from ... I think we thought of it as more –

**Nicola**   Aspirational.

**Barney**   In a way, yeah. It –

**Nicola**   Not that 'we're fucked', instead more, more ... more 'it can be better'. 'We can be better'. 'Than this'.

**Malcolm**   OK. I have some doubts, but if you think so then ... then go for it. Let me see it.

**Nicola**   Coolio. All right. Well in that case, I'm gonna go and check on something.

**Barney**   What?

**Nicola**   Little surprise for you, Barn. Something I've been thinking about. Or some*one*. For tomorrow. Or not, depending. If I've got time. Catch you in a sec.

**Nicola** *hops off, checking her watch.* **Barney** *smiles at* **Malcolm** *and makes to go too.*

**Malcolm**   Yeah, actually Barney, I couldn't just ... for a minute? Could I?

**Barney**   Uh, yeah. Course.

**Malcolm**   (*pause*) How are you?

**Barney**   (*pause*) Fine, thanks.

**Malcolm**   Yeah? I've been thinking. I know everyone's ... I know the rumour mill is in full swing, if that's not ... mixing metaphors. But anyway, you know what I mean. About Mumbai. So I just thought I should say ... well I want to send you.

**Barney**   (*pause*) Oh.

**Malcolm**   I'm giving you Mumbai, basically. Barney.

**Barney**   ... right. (*Beat*). But I don't want it.

**Malcolm**   You don't wa–? Hmm. What?

**Barney**   I don't want it. Malcolm. I've never wanted it.

**Malcolm**   (*pause*) Oh.

**Barney**   I. I didn't think you'd be ... I didn't think you'd want to split me and ... up. You always ... everyone's always ... you know. 'Dream team'. Huh. Why, why / would you –?

**Malcolm**   No, I just thought ... I thought you would want the ... but I was wrong. Clearly.

**Barney**   I just think there are other people. Other more ... you know, great people, Jenny, Josie, I –

**Malcolm**  OK. Yeah.

**Barney**  I just ... I don't want to go there. Malcolm. I'm sorry.

**Malcolm**  No, that's ... Oh, ok. No, that's fine. But you know, fine then, but you know the way things are here at the moment ... well, everyone needs to be doing something. Essentially. All right? There needs to be enough work to justify the staff, so ... yeah, this vodka account. That's something we all need, Barney. Then. In that case. OK?

**Barney**  (*beat. Nods.*) OK.

*Office. Still black, white and grey.*

**Barney** *and* **Nicola** *are just dumping their things down onto their desks.*

**Nicola**  Nice one, Barney-boy. / Get in. Whoop whoop!

**Barney**  No, you led it, well done you. Malcolm looked pleased.

**Nicola**  (*as Barry*) He looked chuffed, he did. Proper happy, know what I mean?

**Barney**  (*as Keith*) Yeah, smashing, mate, that was. On the money, no messing, take that to the bank.

**Nicola**  (*as Barry*) So, fancy a jar? Little tipple, ey? Wet the whistle? Just *aks*ing, mate. Just *aks*ing. A cheeky few before home time? Bit of the old cough medicine before bed, you get me? One down the hatch, no harm done? Doctor's orders. Just to get us going? Just to wind us down. After a day in the rat race. A day on the job? Fancy that? Bit of that do yer? (*Singing, à la* Franz Ferdinand.) 'Yeah, do yer? Do yer, do yer wanna?'

**Barney**  Yeah, all right.

**Nicola**  Ey?

**Barney**   Sounds nice.

**Nicola**   Oh, no, sorry I didn't mean it. Out with Scott tonight.

**Barney**   Oh.

**Nicola**   Sorry.

**Barney**   No, that's all right.

**Nicola**   Come for a bit if you like. It's his friend's birthday or something.

**Barney**   I'm all right, ta.

**Nicola**   They'll take the piss a bit of course, call you gay cause you don't like football, but–

**Barney**   I like football.

**Nicola**   Oh, OK Barney, you like football.

**Barney** *spins a bit on his chair, clicking his mouse as* **Nicola** *packs away.*

**Nicola**   What will you do then?

**Barney**   Dunno, just ... go home and ... you know. Just. Time of year, innit. Depressing.

**Nicola**   I like it. Cosy.

**Barney**   Leave work, already dark. Cold. Get home. Lights on. Bed early. Fucking hell.

**Nicola**   What colour's January, then?

**Barney**   ... I ... (*shrugs*) ... dunno, don't really ...

**Nicola**   Sorry, I shouldn't have ... know you don't ...

**Barney**   (*pause*) Like ... Ford Cortina Red. And it tastes like a, um ... like a raspberry ice lolly. But with all the flavour sucked out, so almost just ice and it's cold and wet on my tongue and ... and it's at the top, there, and you move down to February and then March, and ... and it sounds a bit like ... (*sighs a heavy, 'can't be bothered' sigh*)

**Nicola**    (*laughs*) Sounds as well now. God. So, like, August could be, um ... (*screams like an excited child*)

**Barney**    Yeah. And, I dunno why, but May feels a little bit camp.

**Nicola**    (*laughs*) Yes! Haha...

I wish I could ... I mean the colour thing I think I ... but the patterns and that, it ... I wish I understood it all a bit ...

**Barney**    Well it ... you – it ... (*pause. Sighs.*) It's like when you picture the days of the week. When you visualise 'the week', what pattern is it?

**Nicola**    I don't ... that's the thing, I / don't really –

**Barney**    Like, mine's diagonally up from left to right, Monday to Sunday, getting steeper at the end. And you have to drop down off it to get back to Monday.

**Nicola**    (*thinks*) Erm, dunno, maybe ... maybe like in a circle. Monday, Tuesday, We- ... And just keep going round and round. Or something.

**Barney**    Well there you go, see, that's ... and any colours?

**Nicola**    No. We-ell. Sunday feels brown.

**Barney**    My Sunday's brown! It's ... there, that's how ... that's it. Except that you actually ... *feel* ... (*trails*)

**Nicola**    Wish I had something like that.

**Barney**    (*shakes his head*) You ... it ...

**Nicola**    Right. (*Beginning to pack up to leave.*) Well, we did good, I thought, Barn.

**Barney**    Yeah. Playing off each. Worked.

**Nicola**    It did work. We work.

**Barney**    We do, we ...

**Nicola**    ... well. Thank you for your *benediction*. (*Smiles, and winks.*)

**Barney**  That today's?

**Nicola**  (*indicating a 'word a day' calendar*) Yup.

**Barney**  Very good.

**Nicola**  So I was thinking ... hmm. I was thinking ... maybe I could take the reins on this one? On the vodka. If that was ... something you thought was ... ok.

(*as Timothy*) You know, have a pop at it, Charles. Good crack, all that, yah?

**Barney**  Uh. Yeah. If ... if that's ...

**Nicola**  I don't mind, though. If you ... it's just a lot of other people, Jenny, Josie, you especially ... I just feel I need to puff up my portfolio. A bit. Whereas yours is so –

**Barney**  No, it ... I mean, yeah. Yes. Of ... (*as Charles*) Yah, you go for it, Tim. Let's nail this fucker. With you all the way.

**Nicola**  (*as Timothy*) Great. Thanks.

**Barney**  Welcome.

**Nicola**  And you'll be there for me, will you? You and your ... well, you know, our little secret weapon. I can rely on it, can I, yeah?

**Barney**  ... of course. Always.

**Nicola**  Hmm. You're so cute, Barney.

**Barney**  Am I?

**Nicola**  How can you not have found anyone?

**Barney**  (*shrugs. Beat.*) Maybe I have.

**Nicola**  Maybe you have?

**Barney**  Maybe I just don't know it yet.

**Nicola**  Yeah, maybe.

**Barney**  Maybe it's them that hasn't found me. I don't know.

**Nicola**  Don't know what?

**Barney**  I don't know what.

**Nicola**  You don't know what you don't know?

**Barney**  No.

**Nicola**  Be in late tomorrow morning. Opticians.

**Barney**  How is it, any better?

**Nicola**  (*rubbing*) Sometimes. God, hope they don't give me glasses. Look like a –

*An office phone rings on* **Barney**'*s desk.*

**Barney**  (*answering*) Hello?

Oh. Hi Scott. It's Barney. You downstairs?

**Nicola**  Put it on speaker.

**Barney**  Hold on. (*Does*)

**Nicola**  On my way down, wait there!

**Scott's voice**  (*off*) All right, see you in a sec.

**Nicola**  Catch you tomorrow, Barn. (*Blows him a kiss and exits.*)

**Barney**  (*pause*) You, uh … everything all right?

**Scott's voice**  (*off*) What's that, mate?

**Barney**  With the wedding and everything, all going ok?

**Scott's voice**  (*off*) Uh, yeah. Think so. Dunno, be honest with you, mate. Just …

**Barney**  Huh. No.

**Scott's voice**  (*off*) Let 'em get on with it. You know.

**Barney**  Yeah, best way, innit.

**Scott's voice**  (*off. Pause.*) You good? Everything, uh …?

**Barney**  Yeah, yeah. You know. Busy. (*Pause.*) Erm, so I'm gonna get / back to –

**Scott's voice**   (*off to* **Nicola**) Hi, you all right?

**Nicola**   (*slightly off*) Give me that. (*Closer; off.*) See ya, Barn! Have a good night!

**Barney**   Yeah. Bye.

*The lines goes dead.* **Barney** *sits looking at* **Nicola**'s *desk.*


*Meeting room. The* **Whisky Taster** *stands waiting. He wears a tartan kilt. His large suitcase sits on the table.* **Barney** *enters.*

**Barney**   Hello. Sorry to, to keep you, um …

**Whisky Taster**   Hallo?

**Barney** *glares at the kilt, and has to steady himself.*

**Barney**   Uh, waiting. I – you … I think you've been dealing with, uh, Nicola? My colleague. She, she'll be … right along. Do you need anything? I could … um …

**Whisky Taster**   Are you all right?

**Nicola** *enters and power walks over, hand extended, holding the vodka with the other.*

**Nicola**   Hello, sir. Nice to meet you. I'm Nicola. We spoke on the phone.

**Whisky Taster**   No.

**Nicola**   Sorry?

**Whisky Taster**   I haven't spoken to anyone on the phone, no.

**Nicola**   Ah, right, sorry, I thought I spoke to … think, think, think, Martin? Or someone? From the distillery? (*Referencing his kilt.*) Oh, look at that. That's beautiful. Do you actually wear that around?

**Whisky Taster** *looks down at his kilt then back at* **Nicola**.

**Nicola**   How was your train down; long?

**Whisky Taster**   Um. Fine.

**Nicola**    Still, First Class, ey. Bit more comfortable. Least we could do –

**Whisky Taster**    / First Class?

**Nicola**    – for such a long journey. Yes, your seat in First Class. Our pleasure.

**Whisky Taster**    Ah. (*Pause.*) I don't know what that means.

**Nicola**    On the … doesn't matter. Just the seat we gave you.

**Whisky Taster**    That you gave me?

**Nicola**    Yes. You sat in First Class, didn't you?

**Whisky Taster**    Ah. I just got on and sat down.

**Nicola**    In First Class.

**Whisky Taster**    I don't know.

**Nicola**    No, that's ok. That's – it's just, that's fine. On your way back though, look at your ticket. It gives you a seat number, and … it's more expensive. But that's the least we can do. Given you've come down. You're staying with someone, is that right?

**Whisky Taster**    … hmm?

**Nicola**    You know people down here.

**Whisky Taster**    …

**Nicola**    I just mean where are you staying in London; where have you come from now?

**Whisky Taster**    Fort William.

**Nicola**    Right, but I mean here, when you got off the train, you went … ?

**Whisky Taster**    I came straight from the station. It took … I wasn't sure of the way.

**Barney**    But you have somewhere to stay, is what Nicola is just checking.

**Nicola**   A relative. I was told.

**Whisky Taster**   (*pause*) Ye-es.

**Nicola**   And whereabouts is that?

**Whisky Taster**   I ... haven't been able to get in touch. Yet.

**Nicola**   (*looks at* **Barney**) Well ... why don't we, uh ... why don't we put you up in a hotel tonight? We'd planned to do that anyway. Just so you don't have to worry, how's that?

**Whisky Taster**   Uh, thank you.

**Nicola**   You're very welcome, thank *you*. And feel free to use anything, just keep the receipts, we'll take care of it. Mini bar. Movies on demand, WiFi, anything like that.

**Whisky Taster**   OK.

**Nicola**   Can I get you anything now? Tea? Coffee? Or something stronger? Maybe not just yet, ey. Lot of tasting to do. And it is 4 o'clock on a Tuesday. Don't want to be hammered by five. By six, hell yeah, but not five.

**Nicola** *laughs. Silence.* **Whisky Taster** *looks confused.* **Barney** *is taking deep breaths, wiping his forehead.* **Nicola** *puts the vodka and three glasses on the table.*

**Nicola**   Right. Well. Here we are. What I was talking to you about. Or whoever. What we wanted you to peruse. Give us some of your pearls. Your language. Your ... *poetry*.

**Whisky Taster**   Huh?

**Nicola**   The vodka?

**Whisky Taster**   Vodka?

**Nicola**   Yes. (*Tapping it.*) Here.

**Whisky Taster**   Vodka is not what I do, young lady; I do whisky.

**Nicola**   Yes. Exactly. That's exactly my point. That's what we want. We want this vodka to be like whisky. We're changing it you see. Vodka. We're changing it. So. Yeah. (*Pause*) I'm sorry, what's your job title again? At the distillery?

**Whisky Taster**  Which distillery?

**Nicola**  Uh. I don't – your distillery. The one you work for.

**Whisky Taster**  I don't work for a distillery.

**Nicola**  Oh. Sorry, I ... we were – your people, they told us about you.

**Whisky Taster**  My people?

**Nicola**  Yes, they said ... they told me you were the best.

**Whisky Taster**  I ... it's – it can be difficult to describe what I do. There are no set people I work for. You know.

**Nicola**  Right. I see. Ok. Well, shall we sit down and have a drink of this? Hmm?

**Whisky Taster**  (*noticing* **Barney** *growing increasingly unsteady*) Is he all right?

**Nicola**  Barney?

**Barney**  Y-yes, yeah, I'm –

**Nicola**  Sorry, you'll have to get used to these creative London types. I'm sure you've never seen the like. Actually, sorry, I didn't catch your name.

**Barney**  I'm sorry, I'm, I'm, I'm really ... would you – would it be possible for you to, to ... take that off. Or –

**Whisky Taster**  Huh?

**Nicola**  Barney?

**Barney**  The – your kilt. Sorry, I'm ... I'm really ... no, forget it.

**Whisky Taster**  Take it off?

**Nicola**  He's joking. Barney, stop messing around. (*Laughs.*)

**Whisky Taster**  Is he all right?

**Nicola**   It's fine. Barney feels things more than most
people.

**Whisky Taster**   Huh?

**Barney**   Nick.

**Nicola**   He has a weird thing with colours.

**Whisky Taster**   With colours?

**Nicola**   He feels them?

**Whisky Taster**   He ...

**Barney**   It doesn't matter. Just –

**Nicola**   Synas ...?

**Whisky Taster**   ... *feels* them?

**Barney**   Honestly, it, it, it, it –

**Nicola**   Synanasthe ...? I can never – but that'll be why,
you see. (*Pointing to the kilt.*) All of them. Sends him a bit
loopy. Although at least they're straight lines. Doesn't like
squiggles; says circles 'sound' funny. Ignore him, he
normally calms down after a bit.

**Whisky Taster**   I'll take it off if it's giving you migraines,
sonny.

**Nicola**   No, don't worry.

**Whisky Taster**   But I must warn you I do wear it in the
fashion for which it was traditionally intended, if you get my
drift.

**Nicola**   No, this is silly. Barney, stop being a knob.

**Barney**   I'm not being a knob.

**Nicola**   (*laughs politely to the* **Whisky Taster**) I am so sorry.
Look, basically what we're trying to do is reinvigorate the
culture of drinking vodka, starting with the way it's
branded. Do you drink vodka?

**Whisky Taster**   No.

**Nicola**    And there you are, see? We want people like you to drink vodka. Drink vodka the way you would drink whisky. OK? So what makes you not drink vodka? See, I think it's because, to a man such as yourself, a cultured man, the culture of drinking vodka is not something that appeals. We're not some freezing eastern bloc shit hole, it isn't ingrained in our national, uh, conscience that it's a cheap fuel alternative. The only thing ingrained in our conscience about vodka is the branding. And so we're going to change that. For example, I know. Let's play a game. (*Gesturing a seat.*) Please.

**Whisky Taster** *sits*.

**Nicola**    (*sits*) Let's play some word association. What other words come into our head when I say the word 'Russia?' Hmm? Anything, however obvious or stereotypical. If we go round, and just the first thing that we think of. I'll start. Uh. Ballet. Barney?

**Barney**    Um. Red.

**Nicola** *offers vodka over to the* **Whisky Taster**.

**Whisky Taster**    . . .

**Nicola**    Snow. For example. Barney?

**Barney**    Cold war.

**Nicola**    Wolves.

**Barney**    Submarines.

**Whisky Taster**    . . . erm . . .

**Nicola**    First thing that comes into you head. Missiles.

**Whisky Taster**    Dostoevsky.

**Barney/ Nicola**    Great.

**Whisky Taster**    Stalin.

**Nicola**    Good one. Uh, red and green army uniforms.

**Barney**   A sort of . . . clunky, metallic sound . . .

**Whisky Taster**   . . .

**Nicola**   Dolls that slot –

**Whisky Taster**   Chekhov –

**Nicola**   – inside each other – yes, very good.

**Barney**   Your breath in the air . . .

**Nicola**   Ice skating.

**Whisky Taster**   Chess.

**Barney**   Clapping your, your gloves together to keep warm
by a, a –

**Nicola**   Pulling an envelope out / of your jacket in secret . . .

**Barney**   – by a burning barrel.

**Nicola**   You see it's these things that all vodkas brand
themselves on in this country. Old Russia. Old women with,
with, with headscarves. Any more?

**Barney**   Rachmaninov. Stravinsky. Tchaikovsky.

**Nicola**   Good. Any more?

**Whisky Taster** *thinks. Shifts in his seat, looks very
uncomfortable.*

**Nicola**   You're very tired. I'm so sorry, you've come all this
way, and you haven't even managed to dump your things
yet. Why don't we get that hotel sorted for you, yeah? Then
maybe start proper tomorrow morning or something?
Sound like a plan? OK?

**Whisky Taster**   . . . OK.

*The roof.* **Nicola** *and* **Barney**. **Nicola** *smoking.* **Barney** *hands her a mug of coffee, keeping one for himself.*

**Nicola**  Jesus H. Sorry, Barn. Weirdo or what. Shit. Shit! Half way through the week and we've got fuck all.

**Barney**  You never know, he could still be useful.

**Nicola**  Hmm. Well if he ain't, I'll send him home. Can't have him just leaking money in a fucking hotel, Malcolm'll go nuts. (*takes a sip of her drink. Squirms.*) Yuk. The fuck? This one of your instant shits?

**Barney**  Don't start. Can't stand the posh stuff; too strong.

**Nicola**  Christ, need to grow a pair, Barn.

**Barney**  'Grow a ...' What are you, some eighties, ball breaking, shoulder-padded fucking –

**Nicola**  Just saying.

**Barney**  What? Saying what?

**Nicola**  All right, calm down, drink your piss.

**Barney**  Can't stand 'just saying'. No, you are *saying*. You are saying something.

'I'm going to stab you. What, I'm just saying'.

**Nicola**  All right, Barney, I get your point –

**Barney**  'We will fight them on the streets and on the beaches; what, I'm just saying.'

**Nicola**  All right!

**Barney**  (*sips his coffee. Beat. Smiles at her.*) Oy. You'll like this one.

**Nicola**  What?

**Barney**  'I wish to wash my Irish wristwatch'. Go.

**Nicola**  (*attempting the tongue-twister*) I wish to wash my Irish wist – my Irish wristwash. Watch. I wish to watch my iwish wish wash – *fuck*!

**Barney** *laughs*

**Nicola**   Good one, that. (*Smokes*.) So, how's it going, 'blue, silver, and gold', any thoughts, new ideas? Anything I can feed through to Creative, get them off my back.

**Barney**   Yeah, some, just thinking of, uh ... you know, types of music. Images. Got some copy suggestions. It's coming.

**Nicola**   Like what, what music?

**Barney**   It sounds ... they sound like a piano. I think. At the moment. Quite soft and sad.

**Nicola**   Fucking hell, Barn, we don't want to depress them into drinking vodka.

**Barney**   I'm on it, don't worry.

**Nicola**   (*beat*) I wonder if it's ... I dunno, I don't wanna push you or nothing. But. I don't know. You say you try not to think about it but it seems that, like, if only you ... kind of ... did. Start thinking about it. Started seeing. Everything. And hearing and tasting everything, a bit more. Then you'd find it easier. Maybe.

**Barney**   It ... it doesn't work like that.

**Nicola**   OK. OK. It's just–I'm sorry. It's just Malcolm was laying it on thick. You know. About how important this one is. And whether we can ... 'up our game'. Type thing. That's all.

**Barney**   (*beat*) I'd like to. I would. I'm just ... you can't, erm ... 'control'. What they'll make you feel. And there are things that I ... that I'm not sure I want to. Feel.

**Nicola**   (*beat. Nods. Smokes*.)

**Barney**   So anyway, come on, then, let's see 'em.

**Nicola**   No. Fuck off.

**Barney**   What. Bet you look cool. Intellectual and savvy and –

**Nicola**    See, you're already taking the piss, no.

**Barney**    I won't. Promise.

**Nicola** *sighs. Takes out a pair of glasses from her pocket and puts them on.*

**Barney**    Awh. They look good.

**Nicola**    Don't lie.

**Barney**    Seriously. I think you look ... dunno.

**Nicola**    Like –

**Barney**    Pretty. (*Small pause.*) Well, you know ... for ...

**Nicola**    Mm. Well. I wanna get contacts instead. Not having fucking speckie-four-eyes on all me wedding photos, Jesus.

**Barney**    (*laughing*) 'Speckie-four-eyes'.

**Nicola**    (*laughs*) I mean it.

Trying to get flowers sorted for the church.

**Barney**    Oh yeah.

**Nicola**    Dad's going all out.

**Barney**    OK.

**Nicola**    Do you, uh ... no. S'all right.

**Barney**    What?

**Nicola**    Na-ah.

**Barney**    Go on.

**Nicola**    Nah, it's silly.

**Barney**    Fuck's sake.

**Nicola**    Well. Erm. I wondered if you, like ... I dunno. With your 'thing'. If you had, like ... I dunno. A colour for ... you know. For feeling ... you know –

**Barney**   What?

**Nicola**   For. Love.

**Barney**   ...

**Nicola**   Or ...

**Barney**   Not ... erm –

**Nicola**   Just struggling to pick flowers, you know. Thought it might be funny. Get your take on it, type thing. Carnations. Lilies. Orchids. You know.

Sorry. I know you don't like ... talking about – or ... sorry, Barn, I –

**Barney**   No, no, no, it's ... not – I don't um / ... I don't, like –

**Nicola**   Seriously. Enough. Honestly. I'm sorry. (*She smokes*) Do make me feel cleverer, though. Having these on.

**Barney**   You don't need them to be clever, Nick. You're very clever.

**Nicola**   Most people don't think so.

**Barney**   They're knob heads.

**Nicola**   Scott never thinks of me as being par-tic-u-larly clever. Not in ... you know, not in that way. Anyway.

**Barney**   Well ...

**Nicola**   (*beat. Smokes.*) Come round dead quick, hasn't it? Mumbai. When it first got mentioned I remember thinking, 'fuck, that's ages away'. But ...

Christ, getting wound up about the whole thing, now, need to calm down.

**Barney**   Why you getting wound up?

**Nicola**   Why do you think?

**Barney**   There's / no point.

**Nicola**   Why is anyone? Because I want it. What do you mean, no point?

**Barney**   If it's meant to be, it's meant to be.

**Nicola**   (*smokes. Beat. Watches him.*) That's what people say to people when they don't think something is going to happen. You don't reckon I'll get it.

**Barney**   I reckon there –

**Nicola**   (*laughs, a little passive aggressively*) Right. Well . . . maybe you . . . well –

**Barney**   I'm just saying, there are so many people up for it, people who've / been here longer, who are slightly more –

**Nicola**   Well, you know, it's all right for you, Barney, you're safe aren't you, they 'need' you, never gonna let you go, / but some –

**Barney**   Oh. Whatever.

**Nicola**   – of us, some of us aren't as indespensi-what's-it, as you, some of us have got to try and make ourselves as . . . I mean, seriously, look at me. I've only ever been in this one company, working my way up. If I'm not here then I won't be bloody anywhere.

**Barney**   Shut up. You're brilliant. They won't let you go, Mumbai or no Mumbai.

**Nicola**   Well . . .

Be strange, wouldn't it. If they did split us up.

**Barney**   (*pause*) . . . hmm . . .

**Nicola**   Would you miss me? In the ridiculously unlikely event that I went; Mumbai.

**Barney**   (*slight disbelief at the question*) Would I . . . ? (*It catches in his throat.*)

**Nicola**   (*playfully*) Would you? Would you, Barn? Having to find someone else? Would you miss me?

**Barney** *tries to smile, but can't. Shuffles his feet. Looks at her. Looks around. Looks at his feet. Looks at her.* **Nicola** *notices his reaction. She smokes. Silence.*

**Nicola** Can't wait for the weekend, now.

**Barney** Yeah.

**Nicola** I'm gonna get off my tits. I reckon. Off My Fucking Tits.

*Meeting room.* **Barney** *seated.* **Malcolm** *up and down. Notes across the table.*

**Malcolm** I mean I do think you're right. I think what Nicola is trying to do, and you, I think it's dead right. Instead of trying to squeeze into an already, um, bulging-at-the-seams market, shifting the goal posts entirely. Tapping a new reserve. Cool, ok. I just wonder ... I mean, it's, huhuhu ... it's the one thing, in this age of, in this time of economic ... it's the one thing that is sustaining itself–not only sustaining itself, flourishing, and it's flourishing amongst you lot, because ... well. You're still rich, aren't you. By the standards of ... and your disposable income, it ain't going on houses, is it, because you can't. So...

**Barney** So you're saying ... you still think we're going the wrong way –

**Malcolm** I'm just asking you to keep asking yourself that question, OK? You, why do *you* drink? If ... I hate this kind of–and, Jesus, I know you do as well, the definitions, the wanky terms, but ... OK, but for the sake of argument, me, my lot? (*References himself.*) Generation X. Yes? And you. Generation Y. OK? You, you lot, 'Gen Y', are we missing a drink by not marketing this vodka to you. To ... *Nicola.* Yes?

(*beat*) I mean, OK, that stuff, all that stuff you talked about, with Facebook, and Twitter, I see that. I think that's more like it, that's the right tracks. Huh, not that I've ever understood it myself. Do you ... (*mimes typing*) ... are you into all that, or –

**Barney**   Erm, no, not really.

**Malcolm**   Boggles my mind. Honestly. Huh. Never have a people spoken to each other so often, and yet all it's exposed is an absolute absence of anything worthwhile to say. (*Beat.*) Do you know what, you'll like this, Barney (*flicking through notes*), huh, erm, there was a ... there was one particularly (where is it) one radical Social Darwinist of, of the last ... can't find it, but ... what he–ah, Lapouge. Here. Lapouge. He, um ... he wondered whether drink should be provided free to the lowest rungs of society, in the hope that they might either kill themselves off in drunken whathaveyous, or gradually just become infertile and slowly die out. Backhand eugenics, almost (*laughs*). Though something quite salient. In the idea. That it's almost actually ... that it's, you know ...

**Barney**   ...

**Malcolm**   So, Nicola's doing well, is she? I like Nicola. She's great. Great fun. And I know that you'd want to do anything to help her. And I know you will, because I know you want her to do well. I know that you'll, uh ... 'give her' ... what she needs, in terms of ... in terms of you, Barney. I think that would be fair. If she needs you to.

And, hey, I was only being told yesterday by some of the Execs how 'vital' you are. Barney. How 'key'. So ...

**Barney**   ...

**Malcolm**   I have had some staff come to me and say they can get a little annoyed. Actually. About you and Nicola. About the cliqueyness, and the in-jokes, and what's this, something about characters and, and voices? Just to flag that up now.

**Barney**   ... OK.

**Malcolm**   (*smiles*) OK.

*Meeting room.* **Whisky Taster** *stands.* **Barney** *and* **Nicola** *face him.*

**Nicola**   How was it? Your hotel?

**Whisky Taster**   It was. Fine. Thank you.

**Nicola**   Sleep well?

**Whisky Taster**   No.

**Nicola**   Go anywhere nice last night?

**Whisky Taster**   No. I stayed in my room. Watched some television.

**Nicola**   Cool.

**Whisky Taster**   Musical channels. American. Mainly.

**Nicola**   Yeah?

**Whisky Taster**   Is it what young … is that what you're watching.

**Nicola**   Who?

**Whisky Taster**   You? Young people?

**Nicola**   Dunno. Maybe. I like your jacket, top, thing. Very dapper. Going anywhere nice?

**Whisky Taster**   (*looks down at his jacket. Pulling at it a bit.*) Uh. My daughter, I was …

**Nicola**   Cool, man. Well. (*Nudges the bottle and glass forward.*) Here we are then.

**Whisky Taster** *looks at the vodka bottle, and at* **Nicola**.

**Nicola**   You probably think we're cheating a bit, don't you? Just wanting to short cut it all those years, decades, centuries of your … of the culture of whisky evolving to become this, this –

**Barney**   But actually, no, what we're trying / to do, is, is …

**Nicola**   Exactly, no, we're are trying build it up little by little, softly, softly, that's why we don't want a massive, bling

bling campaign, full of fireworks, we want it to develop, or *seem*, to develop, organically. Even though it's not, even though we're 'managing' it. But I know what you're thinking, 'well, that's still cynical marketing', that's still ... 'grrr, the evils of advertising, brainwashing', but it's not, any more, is it. Barn? It's all changed now.

**Barney**   Because we get it.

**Nicola**   That's it. As consumers, we all get it. We're all so sophisticated, now, we know how advertising works, what they're trying to do. And you know, Jesus, they're not forcing us, we fucking love buying stuff. It's like we're all in on the joke.

**Barney**   Everyone has a favourite advert.

**Nicola**   God, if I hear one more person talk about the new Honda ad I'll eat my own arm. Or that iPhone one. People love teaser ads. They love film trailers. People get excited by good campaigns. They Will Get Excited By This. And to get us started ...

(*nudging the bottle*) ... we just want to know what you think.

(*waits*) We really are very grateful for your time, you know.

**Whisky Taster**   You're not having my time.

**Nicola**   We're ... ?

**Whisky Taster**   You're sharing it with me. But it is still mine.

**Whisky Taster** *sighs a deep breath, like a maestro about to begin conducting.*

So you want to shave off one final layer? See if there's any use left. Well, let's get one thing straight, shall we ...

*He opens up his case and starts unpacking his kit, talking as he goes. A small glass jug, into which he pours from a bottle of spring water. Three green tinted bottles of whisky, lined in a row. Three whisky glasses. He opens one of the whisky bottles and pours a dram each into three glasses.*

**Whisky Taster**    Physicists, and scientists, do not discover anything that is not already there. That was not already created by God, you understand? Newton did not invent gravity, Einstein did not create energy, Hawking did not invent time. MacDiarmid, quote, 'It is a monstrous thing, that earth can be, no more to me than what my thoughts decree'. I Am Not God. Words can never convey any whole truth. But you're right. I am the best. And I am willing to share things with you, you can filter out what you need, condense it, and bottle it, or whatever, but you will respect what it is I have or I won't give you anything. My gift? I can *smell* ... a well made, loved and cared for single malt whisky and *tell you* the proximity its distillery lies from the sea! I can *taste* its age! I can *tell you* in what season it was distilled. And it should, of course, be distilled in winter. (*Pointing to* **Barney**.) Why?

**Barney**    What?

**Whisky Taster**    Winter? Why?

**Barney**    Uh. What? Winter, what –?

**Whisky Taster**    Summer. For the whisky. Is an overbearing mother. Her children are fat, and lazy, and spoilt. Winter? She pushes her children. Hardens them, challenges them, but most importantly, *punishes* them. Unashamed, unforgiving, merciless, but she is honest, and she is fair. Siphons out the weak and rewards the strong. She is Darwinism. She is Nietzsche. Evolution is ruthless. Our distinctly 'human' notions of universal welfare, and equality, contradict the natural order. And nature will not support us, ever, in our quest for fairness and compassion. She'll test every rivet, eye up every bolt, exploit every weak link, striving constantly to show us the fallibility of our idea and bring it down.

(*He smells it, and savours it. He looks at* **Nicola**.) Do you have any idea what it has to go through to get here?

The barley is drowned, and then burnt, crushed, and
mashed, dried, and fermented. The gruel – aye, gruel is
right, for such a gruelling struggle to have a chance to
simply *be* ... the gruel left over is drained into copper stills,
to be boiled and burned then distilled, once then twice,
producing condensation that evaporates into spirit. And
then, then, when you think it's all over, the spirit is sealed,
tight, in a barrel, a cask, and wheeled, into a warehouse,
surrounded by mountains, and forests, and the doors are
sealed, and shut, and tight, where it is to sit, silently, in the
dark, and think, and mature, for years and years and years.
It's like ... sex. Not lovemaking. *Sex.* Beautiful, yet violent.
Pleasurable, but a struggle. Messy. Exhausting. Dangerous,
even? Pushing, pulling, slamming, turning, twisting, hard,
strong, but careful, precise, extracting the tiny little fleeting
thing you need ... and discarding with the rest.

**Nicola**   You said something about distilling; our vodka is
triple distilled.

**Whisky Taster**   ...

**Nicola**   Not just once or twice. Three times. That
something we can use?

**Whisky Taster**   Distillation is, by definition, reducing and
removing. To make the same. It is the uniform for school
children. It is the state restricting the man. Distil too much,
wee girlie, and you'll end up with a bland, characterless
fool. No, it is from our flaws that we truly get our *taste*. Our
flavour. I would imagine that to be perfect were to be very
bland indeed.

**Whisky Taster** *slides them each a glass along the table, and one
for himself.*

**Whisky Taster**   We start with Glenfiddich. A Highland
whisky. Less peaty than some. More flavoursome, perhaps,
than others. He is light. And approachable. A welcome in.

**Nicola**   Mm. (*Making to sip.*)

**Whisky Taster**   NOT! Yet ... (*pause. Holds up his glass*.) Take it straight first. No ice. Never ice. Though a drop of spring water after the first sip helps to release the flavours, reduce their inhibitions, so they may burst forth and dance. Now, smell.

**Barney** *and* **Nicola** *smell.* **Nicola** *scowls, and* **Barney** *rubs his head, looking increasingly pained. The* **Whisky Taster** *closes his eyes, and speaks softly.*

**Whisky Taster**   Smell for the wood of the cask ... smell for the smoke from the fires ... smell for the copper of the stills ... the dust on the warehouse floor ... the spray from the sea ... for the years it spent in the dark. For the things it missed, the people born and people died, for the stories told, the wars fought, the hearts broken ...

Now. Taste.

*They take a sip.* **Nicola** *grimaces crudely, but the* **Whisky Taster** *pays no attention.*

**Whisky Taster**   (*to* **Barney**) What did you taste?

**Nicola**   (*coughing*) Bloody strong. Jesus.

**Whisky Taster**   What did you taste?

**Barney**   A cat asleep in a bookshop ... spring sunshine on white rocks ... erm ... molten iron crawling across a steel floor ... chemistry lesson at school ... little nuggets of gold ...

**Whisky Taster**   (*softly*) That's how you taste whisky?

**Barney**   (*quieter*) That's how I ... taste. Everything.

**Whisky Taster**   (*quieter still*) Well I'll be ...

(*back with the whisky*) Twenty-one years old. Gran Reserve. Rum cask. There is a ... (*sniffs*) ... a floral fragrance. Heather. Slight smoke. But delicate. Not from a fire. Not even a match blown out. Just a match lit, perhaps. The scent of the friction as it strikes. It *feels* ... soft. It ... *sounds* like ... Beethoven.

**Nicola**   Wow. Barney, how cool is this? This is great.

**Whisky Taster**   (*to* **Barney**) What's your name?

**Barney**   Uh. Barney.

**Whisky Taster**   Ach! Your real name. Family name.

**Barney**   Munroe.

**Whisky Taster**   Scottish?

**Barney**   No. Well, I . . . um –

**Whisky**   M. U. N. R. O.

**Barney**   (*pause*) 'E'.

**Whisky Taster**   (*didn't hear*) Uh? / 'E'?

**Barney**   'E'. On the end. Yeah.

**Whisky Taster**   'Dread God'. Clan Motto. 'Dread God'. Not know that?

**Barney**   No.

**Whisky Taster**   Red, yellow and blue.

**Barney**   (*suddenly looking horrified*) W-what?

**Whisky Taster**   Your tartan.

**Barney**   My –?

**Whisky Taster**   Red. Yellow. And blue. Against the red, it's almost purple –

**Barney**   (*holding his head, whispering*) . . . stop . . .

**Whisky Taster**   (*pause*) Where you from?

**Nicola**   (*with the vodka*) Shall we crack this open?

**Whisky Taster**   Your accent?

**Barney**   Uh, yes, northern. I'm. Mansfield.

**Whisky Taster**   You are not Northern. I am Northern.

**Nicola**   I'm from Croydon. Ever been? Don't, actually, it's rubbish.

**Whisky Taster**   (*to* **Nicola**) What's your name?

**Nicola**   Kennedy. Oh, do I have one? Motto.

**Whisky Taster**   (*thinks*) *Avise la fin.* 'Consider the end'.

**Nicola**   What? What does that mean? The end of what?

**Whisky Taster**   Munroe and Kennedy? Like Marilyn and Jack. (*Pause.*) What did your father do?

**Nicola**   What did my father do?

**Whisky Taster**   His job, what was he? His craft, his trade?

**Nicola**   Flowers. He sold flowers on a stall. Could sell anything actually, my dad. Coals to Newcastle. (*Laughs.*) As he used to say. Which I never really got. Why coals to Newcastle? Dunno. Anyway, I take after my mum more, if anything, even though it was my dad who was always there. Always remember the sound of her coming home late from work, her heels across the hall floor downstairs. Used to think she sounded so powerful. Clop, clop. Clop, clop …

**Whisky Taster**   Your family is your cask, it's where you grew and … *became*. Different distilleries choose different types of oak cask to seal the whisky in for eight years, twelve years, twenty-one. Some used to hold bourbon, others sherry, flavours that seeped into the wood. So while the whisky is growing up, and maturing inside, those old tastes and smells from the cask seep back, into the whisky, forming its character. And flavour. We all taste and reek of the cask that reared us. It runs through our blood. Lives in our skin, forever. (*Pause. To* **Barney**.) What did your father do?

**Barney**   Um. P.E teacher.

**Whisky Taster**   Strong? (*Pause.*) You look like him?

**Barney**   Uh, I never thought so, but –

**Whisky Taster**   You must. Act like him?

The soil, its nutrients, its vitamins, its diseases, affect the trees that grow in it. Thus the wood of that tree affects the cask it becomes, and so affects all generations that mature inside it. Shared characters. Shared flaws. In our fibres. Our fabric.

**Nicola**   See, all that. Wood and soil, that's … it's what we're looking for.

**Nicola** *has poured some still water into the* **Whisky Taster***'s glass, swills it around and empties it into the plant, returning and pouring him vodka from her bottle.*

**Whisky Taster**   'That's what you're looking for'.

**Nicola**   Yes. It is. So, fancy a little taste of ours now?

**Whisky Taster** *takes the glasses over to the pot plant and pours the vodka in. He returns and pours whisky from another bottle into the glasses.*

**Nicola**   Oh. OK. Erm –

**Whisky Taster**   Macallan. Matured only in Spanish sherry casks. / It is dark, and heavy.

**Nicola**   I'm sorry, but I would actually like to get on with / tasting this, please. Barney?

**Whisky Taster**   Burnt caramels, honey, raisins. It sounds more like … *Gershwin*. This one. Wild, yet graceful. It is … a movie star. Of the old days. Ages better than anyone else. And versatile. Can play all the parts under the sun. The older expressions are more refined, less wild, less loud, more at ease with who they are. But still … *dazzling* …

**Barney** *and* **Whisky Taster** *drink.* **Nicola** *sniffs it and plonks it on the table. Silence, as* **Barney** *and* **Whisky Taster** *savour it. Staring at each other.*

**Nicola**   Great. That's great. Shall we move on to vodka? Barney?

**Whisky Taster**   (*to* **Barney**) You are … the first child? You have younger brothers?

**Barney**   What?

**Nicola**   (*making to clear away*) Or not. Whatever.

**Barney**   Yes. One brother. Younger, yes.

**Nicola**   I've got four. Older. Only girl in a house full of boys. Imagine. Fucking nightmare.

**Whisky Taster**   Second-hand casks are the best. You know? For maturing their offspring. The first time casks try to mature a whisky, they impart certain impurities, some unwanted aromas, but by the time it comes to trying again, those impurities have mostly gone. Moses was right to cull the first borns.

**Nicola**   I wonder if you wouldn't mind taking a swig of this, please. Then we won't keep you, I'm sure you've got other people you need to go and, um . . . chat. To. So. Would you mind? At least give us a sniff, or something? / Anything?

**Whisky Taster**   (*ignoring her*) A single malt is precious for one reason alone.

**Nicola**   (*slamming it down*) OK. Well if you're not going to try it then / I don't see –

**Whisky Taster**   It is not like the others. Most of what a distillery produces is mixed with what other distilleries produce to create blends. Our quest for perfection. Adding this, taking out that, make us look better, smell better, taste better, make people want us more. We are embarrassed, and ashamed, of our raw selves, and so we *blend!* We blend . . . so that we may blend in. So that we may taste like the others. Blander.

Less unique, but able to fit in. Happy in our duplicity! Safety through mediocrity. But, but!! A single malt is itself. The product of one cask alone. It smells of its imperfections, tastes of its flaws. Smacks of its sins. But proud. Laid bare on a slab. Worts and all. Here I am . . .

Oh, in the days of youth,

Of all torments the most terrible,

Not ... to be ... like others ...

Never to live a single day

Without being painfully reminded

That one is not like others ...

**Barney**   What is that?

**Nicola**   Barney, I don't think we have time, unfortunately, if he isn't / going to –

**Whisky Taster**   MacDiarmid. The poet.

**Nicola**   – help us then we need to start thinking of a Plan B. (*Holding her hand out to* **Whisky Taster**.) Thank you for coming, anyway.

**Whisky Taster**   (*opening up another bottle in haste*) Wait, one more. I want / him to have just one –

**Nicola**   No, I'm sorry, we have to get on / but thank you anyway –

**Barney**   Nicola.

**Nicola**   (*snapping, a little*) – what? Barney?

**Whisky Taster**   (*pouring*) Talisker. Produces some of the strongest expressions in the world. Its power, its *power*, is just magnificent. Raised with brutality on misty Skye.

**Nicola**   After you've gathered your things, Barney will show you out.

**Whisky Taster**   (*looks at her*) All those brothers. Must have been hard to get heard.

**Nicola**   (*smiling wryly*) No point, mister, sorry. I'm not a riddle wrapped in a puzzle trapped in an / enigma like this one. You won't find anything here.

**Whisky Taster**   One bottle amongst many on the shelf, just sat waiting for some –

**Nicola**   I'm not on the – wanna know who's on the shelf? Barney is. Yeah, your boy there, I've been picked up though I'm afraid. So, sorry about that.

**Whisky Taster**   (*continuing, with his glass*) The longer a whisky matures, the more flavoursome it becomes. The stronger its character. But it needs the strength that comes with age; otherwise ... it's so hard, so hard.

**Nicola**   Beautiful, have a safe journey back, Barney, see you in five.

**Nicola** *leaves.* **Whisky Taster** *stands, holding the glass out. He lowers it slowly.*

**Barney**   If, um ... if you'd like to give an invoice to Eve on the front desk, we'll make sure you receive payment in the form of a cheque at the end of this month.

**Whisky Taster**   Do you love her?

**Barney**   (*pause*) Al-alternatively, if you'd care to post one plus expenses –

**Whisky Taster**   She knows. You know ...

What colour is she, I wonder.

**Barney**   ... (*shakes his head increasingly pained*) ... no ...

**Whisky Taster**   (*beat. Awkwardly.*) I. Haven't seen my, uh ... daughter. In quite some ...

I'd like to ... do that. Before I go ...

**Barney**   Well then ... feel free to, uh ... to stay. A bit. A while. If you'd like.

**Whisky Taster**   (*beat*) You know, the thing about a gift ... is that it's something you are given. Not something you necessarily asked for or wanted. Right?

**Barney**   (*beat*) A 'gift'? Where's the 'gift' –?

**Whisky Taster**   Where they all are. Wrapped up, in a box.

**Barney**   This is no 'gift', it ... it ...

(*looks at the kilt, and then grabs hold of his head. Eyes closed ...*)

It hurts. It hurts to feel these things when I do it. There's too many of them, that's why I try to keep it shut, there's just too many of them ...

**Whisky Taster**   (*watches him. Beat.*) They say, as babies, we can smell our mother's anger, taste her words. Like animals. But as the brain develops, the senses separate from one another. Or are supposed to. To make life ... a little easier. Perhaps. But it's still all an illusion. Our brains transfer everything into something else; the only thing that is truly real is silence, and darkness.

(*Beat.*) Have you ever just thought about ... untying the bow. And letting it go?

**Barney**   I can't ... I can't ...

**Whisky Taster**   You can.

**Barney**   Once it's out, once they're all out, that's it, I won't be / able to ... to put them ...

**Whisky Taster**   Ssh ... ssh ... it's all right. I know. It's all right.

**Barney**   I'm too scared. I can't ... to feel all of those things, I just can't ...

**Whisky Taster**   'In the heart of the world,

Like a knife, quivers this truth.

All that lacks love ... lacks life.'

Do it, son. I know you can do it ...

**Barney**   (*long pause*) We're also able to make a, a BACS transfer direct, though, um ... uh, be warned, once it shows on your account, it will still take between three and five working days to clear.

*Beat. Colours start bleeding out across the room, as though escaping from the* **Whisky Taster***'s kilt. Only a little at first. And then more ...*

*Office. There a noticeably many more colours around.*

**Barney** *stands, holding two cups of coffee, waiting.*

**Nicola** *strides in, wearing a bright red dress.*

**Nicola**   Evening, Barney-boy.

**Barney**   Hello, Nick. Good day? How was everything in finance, how's data, they all right? They 'on message'?

**Nicola**   Well apart from me not giving them a single idea of what we're going to need yet, they're fine. How did you leave it with Crazy McFucked yesterday, send him packing?

**Barney**   Erm. No. I said he could stay a couple more days.

**Nicola**   Barney!

**Barney**   It's fine.

**Nicola**   Why? I'm running this one, I'm the one who has to account for all the money he's pissing up the bloody wall, and for why?

**Barney**   He could still be useful, he –

**Nicola**   Yeah, to you maybe. This isn't therapy, Barn.

**Barney**   Ther- ... yeah, I kn- ... what?

**Nicola**   Anyway. So. (*as Timothy*). Ready to does some blue-skying, Charles, bang our head's together, all that, yah?

**Barney**   (*as Charles*). Totally man, of course, let's brainstorm, incentivise, yah, let's get wet in an ideas shower, great.

**Nicola**   Thanks for suggesting this.

**Barney**   What?

**Nicola**    Pulling a late one.

**Barney**    Well, you know, it's you who's doing it with me, I'm not alone.

**Nicola**    No, I know, but ... you know. It's my head that's on the block, really, and ... well, I'm just saying thanks for sacrificing your night.

**Barney**    S'all right. What else am I going to do? (*Handing her a mug of coffee.*) Here.

**Nicola**    Christ. You're perky tonight.

(*sips her coffee. Almost reels back from its strength.*) What the hell? Barn!

**Barney**    Yeah, all right. S'no biggie.

**Nicola**    Look at this, the real thing at last, wow! It's got flavour and smell and everything.

**Barney**    (*looking at his coffee.*) S'nothing. Just. Giving it a try.

**Nicola**    Is this ... is this him?

**Barney**    Who?

**Nicola**    You know who, what's happened?

**Barney**    What, nothing's happened.

**Nicola**    You wanna be careful, this stuff, might give you a headache, not used to it.

**Barney**    Nah, I'm fine, I'm good to go, I've got loads of ideas.

**Nicola**    Really? Wicked!

**Barney**    Yeah, I've been thinking more about the blue, in the 'blue silver gold', I think it's really electric, really modern, like it's glows, like it's buzzing, you know?

**Nicola**    I've got some music that thingy sent up to me, see / if anything feels right to you.

**Barney**    And the silver's not like, erm … erm, erm, erm, shit what do I mean, what do I mean? Terminator 2, that guy, the one that melts, metal! It's not metal, it's more like, uh, glitter, Glitter spray. The texture of it. Like it sparkles.

**Nicola**    Hmmmmyeah, all sounding a bit …

**Barney**    What?

**Nicola**    I dunno.

**Barney**    What?

**Nicola**    Barney, I dunno! I'm thinking. I mean it feels a bit modern, trendy. We've got to keep it classy. Up market.

**Barney**    OK. OK, yeah, OK.

**Nicola**    Listen to this one.

*Classical music/ instrumental film scores play from **Nicola**'s computer. They listen.*

**Nicola**    Blue, silver and gold?

**Barney**    Er. Dunno. Maybe. No, it's like loads of them, it's like everything. Purple, yellow, turquoise, cream. Cream! That's quite a good id- … actually, no, I've / gone off it.

**Nicola**    Hold on, hold on, got loads more.

**Nicola** *presses play on another one. They listen.*

**Barney**    I like your dress, is it new?

**Nicola**    No, dead, old.

**Barney**    Is it?

**Nicola**    Seen it before.

**Barney**    Have I?

**Nicola**    Barney, would you listen?

**Nicola** *skips and plays another one. They listen.* **Barney** *starts to struggle. Close his eyes, and cover his ears, sitting down. She presses stop.*

**Nicola** This is him, this is. Your mate, from across the border. He's like a piece of fucking kryptonite, he's broken you.

**Barney** No, it's ... I'm just ... it's like it's all really loud, it's like it's all too, too –

**Nicola** It's not really loud, it's fine –

**Barney** Hold on, please, wait, just ... I just need a minute to get used ... I just need a minute, OK. It's hard.

**Nicola** (*beat. She sits. Watches him.*) Shit. Shit, we haven't got anything, have we?

**Barney** What?

**Nicola** We're screwed; we've screwed up. Haven't we? I've screwed up. It's / Thursday night, and we're nowhere, we're just –

**Barney** No. No, we have things, we have the 'exclusive' thing, the, the ... no, we've got stuff. We just ... I just need to ... (*sighs*).

**Nicola** (*beat*) Oy.

**Barney** What?

**Nicola** 'Eleven benevolent elephants.' Go.

**Barney** 'Eleven benevolent elephants, elephen, eleven benelephant, benevolent elovents.' Shit.

**Nicola** (*laughs*) Never mind. What does benevolent mean?

**Barney** Uh. Kind. Well meaning.

**Nicola** Urgh, knew you'd know it. So clever.

**Nicola** *pours* **Barney** *a glass, walking it over to him.*

**Nicola** Come on.

**Barney** I'm all right, ta.

**Nicola** Drink it.

**Barney**    I have drank it, Nick. Just –

**Nicola**    Drink it again.

**Barney**    (*pause. Drinks.*)

**Nicola**    Well?

**Barney**    (*squinting with the strength of it*) Loads of things.
Loads of . . . so many things . . .

**Nicola**    Well tell me them. Not cats in bookshops or school
chemistry lessons? You're not holding out on me, Barn, are
you?

**Barney**    What? What do you / mean, no.

**Nicola**    Because this is mine and not yours?

**Barney**    Nick, how can . . ? No, how can / you even –

**Nicola**    All those things you said and felt and tasted in
there with him; all those things you *always* taste and feel and
this leaves you just fucking numb, does it?

**Barney**    What do *you* taste, Nick? How about what you
bloody taste.

**Nicola**    (*pause. Quick sip. Sighs.*) Weekends in Southend with
my dad. Saturday afternoons in Halfords and B&Q.
Running up the stairs in my slippers. The Champagne Bar
at St Pancras. Bonfire night.

**Barney**    Really? Well that's –

**Nicola**    No. I don't taste that.

I don't taste a fucking thing.

Just booze.

*Silence.* **Nicola** *drinks. She looks around.*

**Nicola**    Reckon we're the last ones here?

**Barney**    At this time, uh yeah.

**Nicola**    (*beat*) I can't believe I've messed this up. Absolutely
fucking typical.

**Nicola** *presses play on another piece. She sits and listens. Staring off. Taking the odd sip of vodka.* **Barney** *watches.* **Nicola** *presses stop. Silence.*

**Barney**    OK. OK. Come on. How about ... bah, bah, bah ... OK, just thinking a bit left field, for the sake of shits and giggles, heading in the same direction, just, just switching lines. East coast instead of west coast. What about we go a bit ... I dunno, like –

**Barney** *plays* Lily Allen's *'The Fear' from his computer.*

**Barney**    Like just a shade younger, like ... you know, like funkier, and ...

**Nicola**    (*listens a little*) You hate this, though. You –

**Barney**    I know, I know, I know, but think Camden market, think Canal Street think ...

**Nicola**    We're not Magners, Barney, this isn't gonna be a party in your apple orchard, it's have a quiet sip when you're on your own.

**Barney**    (*presses stop*) True enough. OK. Well (*searching*), erm ...

**Nicola**    Get enough of that from my niece, anyway. Loves Lily Allen. Far too young.

(*beat. Sips the vodka. Starts half singing lyrics from 'The Fear' to herself.*)

'I don't know what's right or what's real, any more ...

... don't know how I meant to feel ...

**Barney**    Chhh-Charlotte?

**Nicola**    Gemma.

**Barney**    Gemma.

**Nicola**    Fuck is Charlotte?

**Barney**    Dunno. How old now?

**Nicola**    Uh?

**Barney**    How old is she?

**Nicola**    Um. Nine. Or … yeah, nine. Jesus. Fuck.

**Barney**    All grown up.

**Nicola**    I know. Still, you joke, but … fucking hell. It's like, the things she wears and things. It's just, it's mad. Got a mobile phone, and –

**Barney**    Joking.

**Nicola**    – everything. No, I know.

**Barney**    Nine. Who's she gonna call? 'Don't know they're born'.

**Nicola**    Uh?

**Barney**    Just. What they say, innit.

**Nicola**    (*playing with it in her mouth*) ('Don't know they're born').

Wants to be famous. Reads *Heat*. And the rest of them. Then again, so do I, so can't …

**Barney**    (*tuts*) Terrible. Why? Why do you read them? Get a newspaper.

**Nicola**    Boring.

**Barney**    Learn things. The world …

**Nicola**    (*mocking*) 'Learn things. The world'.

(*drinks*). What did you wanna be? That age.

**Barney**    Uh, an account handler at a prestigious London advertising agency of course.

**Nicola** *laughs*

**Barney**    Dunno. Maybe a teacher. Or writer. Studied journalism. But can't remember why.

**Nicola**   I wanted to be a dancer. I should have been a dancer.

Never give my kid a mobile.

**Barney**   (*beat*) God. Guess you'll be ... you know. Having them soon.

**Nicola**   Yeah. Guess. (*Pause. Solemnly.*) Yeah, I guess. Jesus. When did that happen? (*Beat. Shakes her head.*) Fuck, I'm getting *married*. Still feel about sixteen. It wasn't that long ago when I was just ... sixteen.

**Barney**   Still, you know, Jesus. Got, I've got friends, family, back at home, who ... everything. Have ... house and ... car and ... pension schemes, it's ...

**Nicola**   See, that's the problem, I'm surrounded by all my friends from ... they've all been in this position for bloody ...

(*as Timothy*) 'Not like us, ey? Career, career.' Huh. (*Pause.*) Suppose that's one of the reasons that ... why I feel that it's ... time to ...

**Barney**   Well. You shouldn't feel like you have ... I don't know, have to rush. Everything happens ten years later. In London. Seriously. Thirty-five down here is, is twenty-five everywhere else. House, marriage, kids, it's ... it's all relative.

**Nicola**   (*pours herself a drink*) Just goes so fucking fast, man. Pisses me off.

**Barney**   I know. I know. Little things. Like my skin is starting to just look ... really *old*. Like the stomach I'm developing, I just look –

**Nicola**   What? Fuck off, you skinny bastard.

**Barney**   I'm just ... I'm saying that I can, I really ... and, like, even though I'm not, well I am a little bit, but some of the guys I know, my age, they're going there (*points to his* *hairline*), and I'm like, really? Is that it already? Mid twenties and your body is already starting to fucking … Wind Down.

**Nicola**    You can talk; it's my fucking eye sight that's going.

**Barney**    No better?

**Nicola**    (*rubbing her eyes*) A bit. Maybe.

**Barney**    Do you know what pisses me off? That boys, that lads, they hit their sexual peak at, like, seventeen. *Seventeen*. And, you know, without giving too much away, I Fucking Wasted mine. To be frank.

**Nicola** *laughs*.

**Barney**    Seriously

**Nicola**    Oh Barney. What we gonna do with you?

**Barney**    I don't know.

**Nicola**    Need to find you someone. Jenny fancies you, I bet.

**Barney**    No way.

**Nicola**    You don't know.

**Barney**    I do.

**Nicola**    You never know. I know you never know; you can never tell when / someone –

**Barney**    How do you know?

**Nicola**    I just do, I just know.

**Nicola** *presses play. More music. She presses stop.*

**Nicola**    You know. People often joke about us two. Jenny, and her lot.

**Barney**    What d'you mean? About what?

**Nicola**    You know what, Nick.

**Barney**    No.

**Nicola**    (*mock-sighs*) OK.

**Barney**    What?

**Nicola**    Just ... you know, just joking, innit. Because of working together. And everything. How close, and all that. Funny. (*Beat. Laughs.*) It's funny, isn't it? Can you imagine?

**Barney**    ...

*She plays with her glass, contemplatively. She sings, softly, almost to herself.*

**Nicola**    'Red and yellow and pink and green ...

Purple and orange and blue ...

Now I see a rainbow ... see a rainbow ... see a rain...'

*Silence.* **Barney** *watches* **Nicola**. *Who stares off. And drinks.* **Barney** *begins writing letters on a sheet of paper, top line big, next line smaller ...*

**Barney**    Oy, blind bitch.

**Nicola**    What?

**Barney**    (*holding up the sheet*) Read the top row; let's see how bad you really are.

**Nicola**    What? No, fuck off, I've had a drink, it won't be –

**Barney**    Top line, without your glasses.

**Nicola**    Fuck sake, Barn. Meant to be working.

**Barney**    (*mock-London*) 'Fuck sake, Barn. Meant to be working.'

**Nicola**    All right, Dick Van Dyke, fucking hell.

**Barney**    Come on.

**Nicola**    (*sighs. Tries to focus.*) A. I. P. There.

**Barney**    Very good, next one.

**Nicola**    J. Uh. (Fucking hell.) T. Z?

**Barney**   Y Z.

**Nicola**   No. Where?

**Barney**   That's a Y.

**Nicola**   Well it's cause you write you Y's like T's. Spacker.

**Barney**   Next one.

**Nicola**   Nah. Can't see it.

**Barney**   This bottom one?

**Nicola**   No. D?

**Barney**   No.

**Nicola**   See.

**Barney**   (*stands. Moves closer.*) Now?

**Nicola**   No.

**Barney**   Say when.

**Barney** *keeps edging forward . . . and forward . . .*

**Barney**   Awh, you're taking the piss.

**Nicola**   I'm not!

**Barney**   Now?

**Barney** *moves right in, within reaching distance of* **Nicola**, *who grabs his hand, stands, and pulls him in for a hug.*

**Nicola**   Come here.

**Barney**   What?

**Nicola**   Nothing. Just want a hug.

(*pause. She releases him.*) You're so lovely, Barn.

**Barney**   (*moving away*) Why am I lovely?

**Nicola**   Cause you think I'm clever. And no one else does.

**Barney**   That's not true.

**Nicola**    (*teasing*) What's not true, you think I'm clever?

**Barney**    No, 'that's not true' no one – (*tuts*) fuck off.

**Nicola** *presses play on some more music. They listen.*

**Barney**    This is good.

**Nicola**    Is it?

**Barney**    This is really ... yeah, hold on. Wow! This ... it really fits, the taste, the vodka, but ...

**Nicola**    Is it blue, silver and gold?

**Barney**    No it's ... wow, it's ... really ...

(*beat. Looks at her.*) It's green.

**Nicola**    Green?!

**Barney**    Yeah, but it's perfect – WOW! God, it just keeps coming in bursts. It's, it's so 'deep', it's like lime and emerald and aluminous and think about it, think about it. Forest, nature, the planet the countryside, the earth, like what he said, everything he told us, that's exactly what we're looking for.

**Nicola**    And that's what it tastes like, you sure?

**Barney**    Yeah! Yes! It ... it's perfect.

**Nicola** *squeals and hops over to him, grabbing and spinning him. They laugh.*

**Nicola** *takes hold of his face, and brings him in for a 'smacker' kiss.*

**Nicola**    Awh. Barney. You are amazing, you know that? You really are amazing ...

**Nicola** *moves in to him again. And they kiss. Properly this time.*

*They're suddenly hit by a bright WHITE shaft of light, as the peripheral areas snap to black. The music swells ... and then fades as we fade to black ...*

*The meeting room. More colours. Canvases and posters displaying multicoloured images of models drinking vodka hang or lie around the room. The pot plant is dying.* **Nicola** *stands facing the* **Whisky Taster**. *She seems quite 'tense'* . . .

**Nicola**    Thank you for coming back.

**Whisky Taster**    Erm –

**Nicola**    I didn't know whether you'd have fucked off home or not.

**Whisky Taster**    Well, I, uh –

**Nicola**    Sorry I was a little bit pissy the other day, it's been a bit of fucking week, if you know what I mean. Sit down.

**Whisky Taster**    I'm all right standing, thank you.

**Nicola**    I think I really would rather you sat down. I think it would good if you relaxed.

**Whisky Taster**    Relaxed –

**Nicola**    Yeah, be good if you could relax. Quite quickly.

**Whisky Taster**    (*beat. Slowly sits.*) . . . right.

**Nicola**    Only I'm on something of a timer, see. And I need your help, I need your advice.

**Barney** *enters. He's wearing some colours. He smiles when he sees* **Nicola**, *almost goes to touch her, but she moves away.*

**Barney**    Hi, Nic . . . (*sees* **Whisky Taster**) Oh. Hello, again.

**Nicola**    Our friend very kindly agreed to come back, Barney; I asked him to come back.

**Barney**    Oh. OK.

**Nicola**    So. If you two lovers wait here, I'll be back with the vodka and then we can get going, can't we? Two ticks.

**Nicola** *leaves. Silence.*

**Barney** *sits with the* **Whisky Taster**.

**Whisky Taster**    How's it going?

**Barney**    (*beat*) Interestingly.

**Whisky Taster**    Interesting is good.

**Barney**    (*beat. Studies him.*) Do you know what I like?

**Whisky Taster**    What's that?

**Barney**    You're gonna find this weird, given my thing with squiggles and things that aren't – but I love, I Fucking Love, the Circle line. On the tube. Because in actual fact, the Circle Line isn't a circle at all, it, it's almost a square. If you want a straight line, then, then that's your line. And you know . . . that map. The tube map, I can really, I really get it. Even though normally the colours, all those colours, would normally send me into a bit of a . . . because they're, because they're so, because they're . . . you know that map, it's . . . it's actually how the world should be. You know? The, the first tube maps, I've seen them, online, they were these accurate, like, to-scale things. But as with, you know, as with everything when you look at it to scale, it, it was a mess. This headache. But the designer, Beck his name was, look him up, he designed – what they called? – uh, like, um, circuit diagrams, things. He grabbed it and, and reshaped it to create the singular most not-to-scale, seriously, huh, most inaccurate map in the world, but by far, *by far*, the most . . . beautiful. Everything is straight. Either horizontal, vertical, or forty-five degree lines only. And picking out colours that, that just feel *right*. That don't blend or wash over each other. The red central line through the middle, that helps the eye to distinguish between north and south. Then the black arrow of the northern line piercing through the middle; east and west. The district line *should* be green, it just should be; a, a poo-like brown for the Bakerloo, it, it just feels right. And I just – I wish the rest of the world could be so, so easily . . . *redesigned*. And compartmentalised. And ordered. So that it . . . so that it *fits* . . .

And I think that's what it's all about, isn't it? I'm starting to realise. Making every . . .

Does ... does that .. ?

(*studies* **Whisky Taster**) How are you today, all right? How was ... ? What were you doing? The other – your daughter. How was that?

**Whisky Taster**   (*pause*) Uh, fine.

**Barney**   Good to see her?

**Whisky Taster**   Uh, I didn't see her.

**Barney**   Oh.

**Whisky Taster**   Uh, she wasn't there.

**Barney**   She wasn't there?

**Whisky Taster**   She didn't show up.

**Barney**   Oh.

**Whisky Taster**   I went back to the hotel. Watched television. Those musical channels.

**Barney**   Right.

**Whisky Taster**   You all seem so ... angry. Why are you so angry with each other?

**Barney**   Erm. Huh. I don't, uh ...

**Nicola** *enters, plonking down the bottle of vodka and a glass.* **Barney** *stands, enthusiastically.* **Whisky Taster** *instinctively follows him by standing. She opens the bottle, pours a glass of vodka and holds the glass out to him. Silence.*

**Nicola**   Well, silly. Have a taste.

**Whisky Taster**   A taste?

**Nicola**   Yes, why do you think I asked you back?

**Whisky Taster**   I wasn't sure.

**Nicola**   But you know why we invited you anyway, why we paid for you to come down, that was explained, I believe; we paid for you to come so that you would taste this.

**Whisky Taster**   . . .

**Barney**   Maybe a glass of water? To cleanse your palette?

**Nicola**   Barney, Malcolm asked to see you at some point today.

**Barney**   He did? Why?

**Nicola**   He didn't say. Probably wants to use you, use your gift, your extraordinary gifts – well you know, don't you, sir? (*Holding out the glass*) Please?

**Barney**   . . . how are you today, Nick, everything ok?

**Nicola**   Yeah, course. Why shouldn't it be?

**Barney**   Just asking.

**Nicola**   I'm fine thanks. Did you get home OK last night?

**Barney**   I –

**Nicola**   Felt rotten this morning. Did you? Absolute hell. Drank way too much.

**Barney**   No, I was fine. Wasn't really that drunk.

**Nicola**   I was. Off My Tits. Sir? Would you like some ice?

**Whisky Taster**   May I . . . may I use the bathroom? Please?

**Nicola**   (*pausing; still holding out the glass. She plonks it down.*) Left out the door, along the corridor, then left, then right.

**Whisky Taster**   (*pause*) Out the door –

**Barney**   / Left –

**Nicola**   Left out the door, along the corridor, then left then right.

*Pause.* **Whisky Taster** *slowly wanders out, opening the door, closing it behind him.*

**Nicola**   I'm not playing games any more.

**Barney**   Nic –

**Nicola**   The presentation is Monday; it's fucking Monday, and –

**Barney**   Are you OK?

**Nicola**   No.

**Barney**   Anything I can do?

**Nicola**   You can get him to taste this.

**Barney**   (*pause*) Are we . . . ? Even going to mention it? Or . . .

**Nicola**   You should go and see Malcolm, Barney.

**Barney**   Huh, it might be to fire me, you never know.

**Nicola**   Don't be stupid, it's probably to promote you, or give you a pay rise. Maybe ask your advice on Mumbai or something, well if he does, please recommend me, all right, please recommend me to go and live in India as soon as absolutely possible.

**Barney**   (*beat*) And. And you'd go?

**Nicola**   Course I would, course I fucking . . . Me and Scott. Fresh start. Brilliant.

**Barney**   You'd take Scott?

**Nicola**   (*sarcastically*) No, Barney, I'd leave him.

*They stand looking at each other.* **Barney** *confused.* **Nicola** *starts opening up and spreading out files. She stops. She looks back at him again.*

**Barney**   Why are you . . . ? (*Pause.*)

**Nicola**   Finish. Your Sentences, Barney. For God –

**Whisky Taster** *returns.*

**Nicola**   That was quick.

**Whisky Taster**   I couldn't find it.

**Nicola**   You couldn't find it?

**Whisky Taster**   No. But –

**Nicola**  Left out the door.

**Whisky Taster**  But that's –

**Nicola**  Along the corridor, yeah? Then left. And then right. OK?

**Whisky Taster**  I no longer need to go.

**Nicola**  (*pause*) 'You No Longer Need To Go'?

**Whisky Taster**  No.

**Nicola**  OK. OK. Well could you take a seat then, please, sir?

**Barney**  Nick, I don't think we need to be so . . .

**Nicola**  (*waits*) Yes, Barney? 'We don't need be so', 'we don't need be so'? (*To* **Whisky Taster**.) Barney does this occasionally, have days where he expects everyone else to finish his sentences, have you noticed, or just trail off; it's to keep you in suspense about his 'amazing', 'profound', 'insightful' thought.

**Barney**  (*sighs*) OK.

**Nicola**  I mean he is clever. He is. And . . . and he helps me, all the time, and it's so lovely of him. It's . . . like last night, we stayed late, to work, and he helped me. But I think it was the wrong direction to go in.

**Barney**  Wrong direction?

**Nicola**  (*to* **Barney**, *now*) It didn't feel right. Barney. Sorry. Erm . . . So, sir, if you wouldn't mind getting started on this, that would be great, that / would be excellent.

**Barney**  Nick, do you think maybe we could have a quick / chat outside?

**Nicola**  Though saying that, there are loads of things that annoy me about him, like supplying words for other people's sentences or correcting them on word use. What was that one you did for me the other day?

**Barney**   I don't / remember?

**Nicola**   I've got one for you. (*To* **Whisky Taster**.) What do you think to our images here, sir? Our models? Don't you think they're very 'heterogeneous'. This lot. Ey? (*Winks at* **Barney**). 'Heterogeneous'.

**Barney**   I don't know that one.

**Nicola**   (*gasping playfully*) What? I have discovered one that Barney Munroe doesn't know? Remember this day! It means 'diverse'. Barney. Diverse. (*Holding the glass out for the* **Whisky Taster**.) Are we ready?

**Whisky Taster**   You remind me a little of my daughter. You know.

**Nicola**   You should see his texts as well; the way he writes his text messages.

**Whisky Taster**   She is very strong willed.

**Nicola**   They're so proper. Full words. Full stops. You used a semi colon once.

**Barney**   Did I?

**Nicola**   Yes, you did. Yes You Did Barney. You must have had to scroll down in the symbols bit and everything.

**Barney**   OK.

**Nicola**   I'm not even sure I know what they're for. (*Laughs.*) Truth be told. Not even sure if I know.

**Barney**   I'm not gonna lie to you, this is all a bit beyond me, this is.

**Whisky Taster**   She won't even see me, now.

**Nicola**   Awh. Little taste of vodka, cheer you up?

**Barney**   You use too many exclamation marks. In everything. Texts, and ... means they've lost all power. / They don't mean anything anymore.

**Nicola**  I like them. Makes everything sound more fun. Cheeky. I use them cheekily. Barney. Ironically. Even. You might say. Perhaps.

**Barney**  Never mind.

**Nicola**  (*laughing*) Winding you up. So easy for me to wind you up.

**Barney**  Yes, it is.

**Nicola**  Barney's very clever, you know. He 'knows things'. He went to university. He sometimes says I'm clever but I don't think he thinks it's true. I can't often understand what he's talking about when he's talking about politics or something like that. Events in history I'm meant to know but don't.

**Barney**  You could know it. It's all there.

**Nicola**  Would you taste this please? Will you / taste this?

**Barney**  If only you took the time to read the paper or watch the fucking news.

**Nicola**  I don't want to watch the fucking news! Why would I want to do that?!

**Barney**  To find out What Has Happened Today.

**Nicola**  I can guess what has probably happened today, Barney. I can guess that things probably Got Worse. I'd guess that things are probably worse today than they were yesterday, but that they aren't as bad as they're going to be tomorrow. I can guess that the hole in the ozone layer probably got bigger. I guess that some starving people probably died because they were hungry. But despite that I'd say that the planet is probably fuller today than it was yesterday. I know that somewhere it rained, somewhere it snowed, and somewhere there was sunshine. I know that a bomb probably went off somewhere. I know that, somewhere, somebody horrible did something horrible to somebody nice!

I don't need to see the news to know that.

**Barney**   You need to see it so that you can change it.

**Nicola**   I Can't Change it, Barney. I just can't. Can you?

**Barney**   (Maybe).

**Nicola**   Huh?

**Barney**   Maybe.

**Nicola**   Well you go and do that, then. Over the weekend. I'll finish the pitch. And you save the world.

(*to the* **Whisky Taster**, *holding the glass out*). Would you taste this please?

**Whisky Taster** *looks at the glass, and then at* **Nicola**.

**Nicola**   Will you taste this, please?

Will you have some, please? Will you have some of this?

Please Will You Taste This?

Will you taste this? Will you? Will you taste this?!! Won't you?! Won't you taste this please?! Will you taste this?! Please! Will you taste?! Will you?! Will you taste?! Won't you taste this?! WILL YOU TASTE THIS PLEASE?!!

*Silence. The* **Whisky Taster** *takes the glass from her hand. She takes a breath, exhausted, as he sips the vodka. Swallows. And puts the glass down.*

**Nicola**   . . . well?

**Whisky Taster**   It's . . .

**Nicola**   Yes? . . .

**Whisky Taster**   Empty. Transparent. And bland.

*Silence.* **Nicola** *nods her head. Gathers her files, the glass, and the bottle. And exits. Silence.* **Barney** *looks exhausted.*

**Whisky Taster**   You know, the smell of the smoke from the kiln that burns the malt dry. At the very start of the distillation process. You can never shake that smell. Always there. There to remind. We all stink of it. And when they prise open a cask that's ready, after all that waiting, the volume of its content has gone down since they sealed it in years before. As has its strength. Its wildness. It evaporated through the cracks in the side, floating up and up, to become nothing but a stain on the ceiling. They say these are impurities, lost as we get older and mature. Flaws that are better off gone. But I'm not so sure. They call it The Angel's Share.

**Barney**   (*pause*) I have a headache.


*Meeting room.* COLOUR *everywhere now.* **Malcolm** *and* **Barney** *are standing –* **Malcolm** *pacing some.* **Malcolm** *could have a green and blue tie-dyed shirt. Possibly even some colourful make-up, lipstick etc. Looking almost clown-like. He's constantly checking the door.*

**Malcolm**   What do you think, going well, going all right?

**Barney**   Erm. Yeah, I . . . yes.

**Malcolm**   Chris is in a good mood. Well, for him anyway, huh. And Nicola's all right on her own, leading him round Creative and everything, she's –

**Barney**   This is her pitch, she's led it, so . . .

**Malcolm**   Yeah, no, course. (*Checking his watch.*) How long have they . . ?

**Barney**   I'd give them another five.

**Malcolm**   OK. OK, cool.

Loads of confidence today, Nicola. Great poise, real commitment, really good. I've been so impressed with her. Really. She's really stepped up, this time. Really proved herself over Mumbai.

**Barney**   (*pause*) Ni- . . . Nicola?

**Malcolm**   Yeah.

**Barney**  You'd send Nicola?

**Malcolm**  Yeah, maybe. If this goes well, with Chris, if she proves herself. Yeah, maybe, why? You don't want it, still, right?

**Barney**  But ... but then we'd still be split up.

**Malcolm**  Well that's OK, Barney –

**Barney**  We're the ... why would you ..? We're the, the team, everyone says, one of the, the best, / so why would ...

**Malcolm**  Well. All good things, and all that. Ey?

**Barney**  Malcolm, I ... / ... I really ...

**Nicola** *can be heard laughing, off.* **Malcolm** *readies himself. She enters, showing* **Chris** *through into the room.* **Chris***, like* **Malcolm***, is very colourful.*

**Nicola**  ... tell me about it. Still means there's no need for a gym membership, is there?

**Chris**  No, I suppose not. (*To* **Malcolm** *and* **Barney**.) All right?

**Malcolm**  Hey, how was it, your little tour.

**Chris**  Yeah, good. Fascinating. Seem to have accumulated a lot of very talented people.

**Malcolm**  Ah, well thanks, you have to, this game. It's a cut throat world out there.

**Nicola**  So, feel free to take a seat and we'll sum up? Barney, do you ... anything you want to add at this point.

**Barney**  ... erm ...

**Nicola**  Nope, OK. Well, as you just saw from our print designs, what we've gone for as the leitmotifs of our campaign we know might seem initially quite unconventional, but it's only unconventional for Vodka. OK? But for other drinks, whisky, wine, gin, certainly, you know, bottled water and ... (*looking at* **Barney**), what were some of the ...? (*Waits a bit – nothing.*) But, yes, as our Planning people outlined, these are images and associations that our consumer base relate to. So, taking the main campaign colour as *green* ... everything you saw, the trees, the model's make-up, the, the idea, the connotations of green being nature. Organic. Healthy. Which is all very much the zeitgeist at, at the moment. So for the bar displays, we have forests, woods, lakes in autumn and in summer. Again full of colour and life, ideas of energy, activity, no snow anywhere. And, uh and on the back of the bottle. The thing we're most proud of. The MacDiarmid poem. Our brand philosophy.

(*reading*) 'Spirit is just this,

Not to be like the others.'

So, uh, emphasising the idea of ... that this isn't for everyone. We're not pretending that it is. It's expensive. It's unique. It's for those who truly appreciate it. Correlating with our key brand points of differentiation, exclusivity, uh ... and speciality.

**Nicola** *clasps her hands, as though finished.* **Malcolm** *watches* **Chris**. *Silence.*

**Chris**  Yeah, it's all very good (*another pause*) ... I thought the key colours were going to be blue, silver and gold. I really ...

**Nicola**  Right, OK. / Erm ...

**Chris**  I really liked that. Is the only thing.

**Nicola**  Yes, well, Barney I know you had some, uh ... it was ...

**Nicola** *looks to* **Barney**. **Barney** *looks like he's going to speak, like he wants to, looking at* **Nicola** ... *but then doesn't.*

**Nicola**  It's just, erm, I felt in the in the end that silver and blue were too cold, too hard. We wanted something warmer

and, and green is so, so current and yet, I mean, green you
... you just don't associate that with vodka, do you?

**Chris**   No. You don't.

**Nicola**   ... I mean, Barney, you're probably better placed
to ... talk about why green.

**Barney**   ...

**Nicola**   Green? Barney.

**Barney**   ...

**Nicola**   Barney?

**Malcolm**   Barney.

**Barney**   (*pause*) ... uh ... just. Quite liked. Green. Really.

*Silence.* **Nicola** *staring confused at* **Barney**. **Chris** *nods, and
begins to leave.*

**Chris**   Well. Thank you very much for all that, we'll be in
touch. Malcolm, as always.

**Malcolm**   Thank you. Chris.

**Nicola**   It's just through here, I'll show you out.

**Malcolm**   Bye.

**Chris**   Bye.

**Chris** *exits, followed by* **Nicola**, *who shoots* **Barney** *daggers as she
goes.*

**Malcolm**   Wow. I mean ... I mean wow, that was, ahuh,
ahuhahaha, that was, yeah, quite something. Barney. I
mean ... I mean, what the fuck?!

**Barney**   What? It was ... it was Nicola's pitch, / I was just

**Malcolm**   You're embarrassing, you're a fucking
embarrassment, do you know that? Both of you. All of you.
All of you! Fucking hell!

**Barney**   Malcolm, I'm ... sorry, I ...

**Malcolm**   (*long laugh*) You can't stand me. Can you?

**Barney**   … erm …

**Malcolm**   It's OK. I don't mind. And I know why. But it isn't my fault I'm where I am, Barney. I can't help that.

**Barney**   Malcolm, I'm sorry, I … I / don't hate you –

**Malcolm**   On the contrary, I offered to promote you, rather heroically, instead of … well –

**Barney**   Well, you … huh, you offered to send me away / from every– …

**Malcolm**   You hate me because of all the things I've had that you will never have; underwhelming, as you might find me. Lacking in any discernible superhuman gift, as I may be. Well I'm sorry about that. I'm sorry I was born into a time that allowed me to succeed and you've been born into one that is going to fuck you over. But do you know what? Even when I *do* give you a chance, you fuck it up.

**Barney**   Malcolm, you're completely wrong, but I don't care enough to want to change your opinion, so –

**Malcolm**   No, see that's the problem, you *do* care. That task I set you, the question I asked you which you have singularly failed to answer, which is why this whole vodka pitch has been wrong from the start, is 'Why Do You Drink?' Your lot. Them. They drink, so that they can forget, that they work all week to earn money, to get to the weekend, to buy drink that helps them to forget that they spend all week working, to earn money, so that they can drink. 'Generation Y', fucking hell yeah, 'Generation Why'. Generation 'why the fuck?' I hand you something on a plate and you piss it away. This account, Mumbai, it's pathetic, Barney, you deserve all you fucking get. Or 'don't get', I should say.

**Barney**   Well. I happen to think that is massively unfair. And even if it were true, I don't blame them –

**Malcolm**   No, I don't blame them, fuck it, if I were your lot, I'd fucking drink. Can't get a house, awh sorry, we've got them all, and shit, sorry, we've spent all that inherited wealth that's been passing down the generations on second homes and cars and holidays. But that's ok, you've been very patient, waiting your turn, but now – oh no! – there's no money left, we spent it, and there's less jobs, crikey, so tighten your belts. I would go away, travel, escape, but you can't really because we did that too much and now the planet needs saving. But the tragic thing is, the real crime, Barney, whatever you hate me for or blame me for, the biggest fucking crime of all is that none of you are angry enough to do anything about it. If this had happened to us, my God, we'd have set the place on fire. We were, we were changing everything, questioning everything, but you lot, God! You just shrug. And follow us. Do what we did. Go to uni still, even though when we went, it *meant* something. And you rent. From us. And pay your taxes, for our pensions and our retirement, none of which you will get to enjoy yourselves. That's why you drink. You're a stopgap. An interval. And the worse thing is you don't even care. But *you*, Barney, I see it, you do care. And you / hate me for it.

**Barney**   OK. OK, erm, so yeah, how is that second home, incidentally? Not going into arrears, I hope. What about your investments, Malcolm, tumble did they? Yeah, yeah, yeah, I really envy you with your 'everything'. But do you know what, actually –

**Malcolm**   I think we're actually done, here, / Barney, all right?

**Barney**   No, I'm pleased that We have Nothing. Because it means in all of this, while you lot stress and fret around, because out of the two hundred grand you made on your house last decade, it's gone down by a tiny fraction, we've lost nothing, because we don't have anything to lose. And I imagine you sometimes probably envy *us* that, / as much as you pity us. All right?

**Malcolm**  Is it all just because of her, you don't want to leave her? Because I'll tell you what, I'll be splitting you up anyway because either you change your mind and piss off to Mumbai, or you're out. So . . .

**Barney**  All that – yeah, all that you've had that we never will, fair enough. So go ahead, I say, send round the bailiffs, lose one of your two cars, repossess and foreclose.

**Malcolm**  Barney . . ?

**Barney**  Foreclose on the whole Fucking Lot of you.

**Malcolm**  Barney, sshh. Listen. (*Pause.*) Go to Mumbai. Or go fuck yourself.

**Nicola** *enters.* **Malcolm** *makes to leave.*

**Malcolm**  You're a bunch of wasters. The whole fucking lot of you.

**Malcolm** *leaves. Silence.*

**Nicola**  Why?

**Barney**  . . .

**Nicola**  Why?

**Barney** (*pause. Trying not to break. Shrugs.*)

**Nicola**  You know, you're not as brilliant as you think you are, Barney. Anyone can be Born with something. But it takes a very different person to make themselves something out of nothing.

**Barney**  I've . . . never wanted anything except for . . . for you to do well, for us to do well. As a team.

**Nicola**  A team? Ha. A team, he says. I'm left drowning in the middle of that just then, waving for help, and he says a team? Well, let me tell you something. OK? It Went Better Than You Think. On the way down, me and him, the things he was saying? Well . . . he liked it more than you think. So I may have saved our asses in this one. Well, my ass at any rate. So . . .

**Barney**   … I … don't know what to …

**Nicola**   Well I don't, I … I don't know 'what to', Barney. What did I do wrong, ey? What am I'm doing, what are we meant to be *doing* Barney?! Ey?! I DON'T KNOW WHAT I'M SUPPOSED TO BE DOING!

**Nicola** *tries to calm, gather her breath.* **Barney** *goes to her and she slaps his chest. He grabs her hand. As she tries to pull it back, she pulls* **Barney** *into her, as they stumble back together, breathing erratically, looking at each other, trying to work the other one out.* **Nicola** *slaps him on the chest again and moves away.*

**Barney**   Ouch.

**Nicola**   Oh yeah right, you fucking weakling.

**Nicola** *slaps him on the chest again.*

**Barney**   Don't. That hurt.

**Nicola**   (*mimicking*) 'Don't, that hurt'.

**Nicola** *puts her hands over her face. Beat. She lashes out at his face.*

**Barney**   Stop it.

**Nicola**   'Stop it'. God! That's one thing I wouldn't miss in Mumbai, your constant whining –

**Barney**   Stop it –

**Nicola**   – and your whinging, it's all … everything about you, it's just so wet.

**Barney**   If it makes you feel better to say hurtful things to me because you feel bad you betrayed your boyfriend, then / go ahead.

**Nicola**   Oh, would you *get over* yourself, Barney! Jesus. It was Absolutely Nothing. OK? Jesus, you're meant to be the smart one, but maybe not. Maybe not.

**Barney**   Maybe not.

**Nicola**  No, maybe not – well, hey, look at me, I'm the one who is moving on, I'm obviously the smarter one.

**Barney**  Yeah, maybe that's right, maybe you are; oh, by the way, Nick, it's because Newcastle Already Has A Lot Of Coal. You fucking idiot.

**Nicola**  (*beat*) Last night. After it happened. I went home. And fucked my fiancé.

Well, I gave him a blow job first, and then I fucked him.

**Barney**  I knew what Green was. I had loads of ideas. I just didn't tell you.

**Nicola**  (*. . . a slight wobble . . .*) . . . And it was a-mazing. To be held by a real man. After . . . after feeling like I was a doll, a doll being fumbled over by a little girl.

**Barney** *tries to brush that off, but it looks like it's broken him. He starts to waver.*

**Nicola**  Now, if you'll excuse me –

**Barney**  I was offered Mumbai.

**Nicola**  . . .

**Barney**  And I turned it down.

*Beat.* **Nicola** *tries to give a 'bothered' shrug, but she slowly starts to break.*

*And then she really does. Clutching at her mouth, bending over.*

*So does* **Barney**.

**Nicola** *allows herself to almost fall to the floor, and sits down.*

**Barney** *gets onto his knees. Holds himself a little.*

*They sit on the floor for a moment, away from each other.*

**Nicola** *tries to gather herself. She slowly stands, brushes herself down, wipes her eyes, and walks uneasily out . . .*

**Barney** *alone. The 'green' music plays.*

*The rooftop. The colourful lights of the city.* **Barney** *and* **Nicola** *stand facing each other, wrapped up against the cold.* **Nicola** *smokes. She looks like she's been crying.*

**Barney**   Was it mutual, or ...

**Nicola**   um ... kind of. More ... more him. I guess.

**Barney**   I'm. Sorry.

**Nicola**   (*tries to laugh, wave it off*) That's ... it's ... huh. It's fine. (It's fine). Back to the drawing board. Ey? 'While there's still time'. Huh ...

Doesn't matter anyway, does it? Won the vodka account. So I got the job. So I'm off. So Fu-fuck it. Huh.

What about you? What will you do? Now. With ... all your spare time and everything.

**Barney**   I. Don't know. Erm. Might actually – I might take up the writing. Thing. Again. Try and do some ... I don't know, articles, or ... short – I don't ... but ...

Might go away. For a bit, first. I've not ... seen anything. I've always been too ... it's always felt like it would be too ... but I ... I think I'm ...

**Nicola**   Oh God, though, you're not going to be one of those are you?

(*as Timothy*) 'Go away and find yourself, yah?'

**Barney**   No, I ... no. Just ...

**Nicola**   Where?

**Barney**   Dunno. The usual. Just ...

Never done Scotland, though. Incidentally. I might start there.

**Nicola**   Maybe you could swing by Mumbai. One time.

**Barney**   Yeah. Maybe.

**Nicola**    (*smokes. Beat. Smokes.*) Or maybe you could just co-
…

(*She stops, losing confidence.*)

**Barney**    What?

**Nicola** *looks like she's about to say it … but then doesn't. She thinks. She looks at him. She smiles bravely. She's really about to say it. But then doesn't. Smokes.*

*Silence.* **Barney** *makes to exit.*

**Barney**    I'm gonna. Head down.

**Nicola**    Told you. Rubbish in the cold.

**Barney**    Yeah. I'll see you –

**Nicola**    So really, you're really just going to go away, and that's it, you're not … I'll nev …

**Barney**    I'm sorry.

**Nicola**    That's OK. What? Why? Don't be, I was just … I wasn't … anything. No, that's OK.

**Barney**    You're just –

**Nicola**    You don't have to. (*Quick beat.*) What?

**Barney**    You're too. Colourful.

*Silence.* **Nicola** *goes back to smoking.* **Barney** *makes to leave again.*

**Barney**    Anyway.

**Nicola**    Yeah. Bye.

**Barney**    (*stops. Beat.*) It's, um. It's white. By the way.

**Nicola**    What is?

**Barney**    You know what. What you asked me that time. Its colour …

Boring, I know. Not bright red or sparkling or ... it's just white. And bright. Really bright. Just a complete absence of anything else. And silent, as well. No noise. And it smells really warm and tastes really young and feels a bit like when you miss a step on the stairs ...

And I cannot tell you how bright it is ...

*Snow starts to fall. Only a little at first, and then more.* **Barney** *looks up, as* **Nicola** *slowly disappears, and the colours from the city, and those all around him, begin to fade back into black, white and grey.*

**Barney** *smiles, as he closes his eyes, and lets the snowflakes fall onto his face ...*

*Lights down.*